JESUS AND HIS WORLD

Jesus and His World

Peter Walker

Downers Grove, Illinois

For Georgie, Hannah and Jonathan,
and for Tom Wright,
friend, mentor and fellow traveller

A scene from the 'Nazareth Village', a reconstruction of 1st-century Nazareth.

Previous pages: An aerial view of modern-day Jerusalem from the south-west, showing Dormition Abbey, the Dome of the Rock and El Aqsa Mosque, Mary Magdalene Church and the towers on the Mount of Olives.

Page one: Fishermen on Lake Galilee.

InterVarsity Press
P.O. Box 1400, Downers Grove, IL 60515-1426
World Wide Web: www.ivpress.com
E-mail: mail@ivpress.com

Published in the United States of America by InterVarsity Press, Downers Grove, Illinois, with permission from Lion Publishing.

ISBN 0-8308-2355-7

Printed and bound in China

Library of Congress Cataloging-in-Publication Data has been requested

P 15 14 13 12 11 10 9 8 7 6 5 4 3 2 1

Y 11 10 09 08 07 06 05 04 03

Contents

Introduction

To understand the real Jesus, we have to make a journey. Jesus lived in a very different world from ours. If we are going to understand him, we have to think our way back into his world. But to get back into his world, we have to be ready for a while to abandon our own. And this can be quite a shock – even for people who see themselves as followers of Jesus.

One of the amazing things about this figure of ancient history is the way his life and story have been transported into very different cultures. We see it in art – the different presentations of an African Jesus, a South American Jesus, the 'meek and mild' Jesus of the Victorians. People have been able to latch onto the story of Jesus and make it their own. They find in Jesus' particular story something universal – the story of Everyman. There are good reasons for this, as we shall see, but the danger is that we begin to

The prow of an Indian fishing boat bears an image of the Virgin and Child.

make Jesus fit our preferred expectations and agendas. We easily make Jesus 'in our own image'. So the same Jesus becomes for some a champion of conservative values and for others a radical who overturns the status quo. This variety pays tribute to the way Jesus' story can resonate with a wide variety of people. But it does beg the question: who is the real Jesus?

The Jesus presented in church is not much better. Stained-glass windows make him seem unreal. They may capture something of the divine, but they lose something of Jesus' humanity. Can this other-worldly Jesus be reconciled with the real 'flesh and blood' person of ancient history? He seems detached, even from the particular issues of his own day. The strange thing is, some people even prefer it this way. They feel quite threatened by the idea of understanding Jesus in his real 1st-century context. They fear a tension between their 'spiritual' Jesus and the historical Jesus. What if the real Jesus turned out to be quite different from the Jesus of their imagination?

There have indeed been some very unhelpful portraits of the 'historical Jesus' in the last 200 years. But the right response is not to abandon history, hiding in some 'spiritual castle' where the rough and tumble of historical reality cannot reach. The answer is to do history properly. And that means not allowing the agenda to be set by those who insist on driving a wedge between so-called 'history' and spiritual reality. This was one of the big divisions that entered Western thought in the 18th century (the misnamed 'Enlightenment'). Historians, we are told, can have no room for miracles or divine activity: 'God' and 'real history' live in two separate realms.

Viewed in this way, the historical Jesus will obviously be explained in

Chinese silk painting of Jesus and Mary Magdalene.

secular terms and the story of his life trimmed to the point where we have no need to speak of God. But suppose for a moment that the Jesus of real history was larger than that. What if the Christian claim just happens to be true – namely that in Jesus we see the activity of God himself, the divine entrance onto the stage of world history? This is an enormous claim, and we shall be examining it in this book. But for now the point is simply this: if it is true, we will need to do history in a different way. We cannot decide in advance what happened, but instead must allow the evidence to take us where it will.

The kingdom of Herod the Great was divided after his death between his three sons, Archelaus, Antipas and Philip. At the time of Jesus, Herod Antipas ruled Galilee and Perea, and Philip ruled Trachonitis. Archelaus was removed by the Romans for his mismanagement of Judea, which became a Roman province administered by a procurator.

Do not be mistaken: what we are doing in this book will meet with resistance in certain quarters. On the one hand, religious sceptics will say Christians cannot write history. On the other hand, some Christians – those people who, one might imagine, would be most keen to find out about 'Jesus and his world' – would rather leave the whole topic alone.

This book, then, is an invitation to go on a journey – to find the authentic Jesus. This will involve going back into his world – or perhaps we should say, into his *worlds*. For Jesus did not live only in the Near East of the ancient world; he also lived in a very particular part of that world, namely the religious world of Judaism. For many of us, both these worlds are totally different from our own, and we need to think our way back into them. We have to do some cross-cultural travel.

This has always been the case. When Luke wrote his account of Jesus, he ensured that his readers placed the story of Jesus both in the world of the Roman empire ('in the 15th year of Tiberius Caesar') and in the world of Judaism ('during the high priesthood of Caiaphas'). People will not be able to understand Jesus correctly, he was saying, if they will not make the effort to enter into these two worlds.

So, in the opening chapters, we set Jesus in the context of the ancient world. But we soon discover that we need to enter more fully into the narrower world of

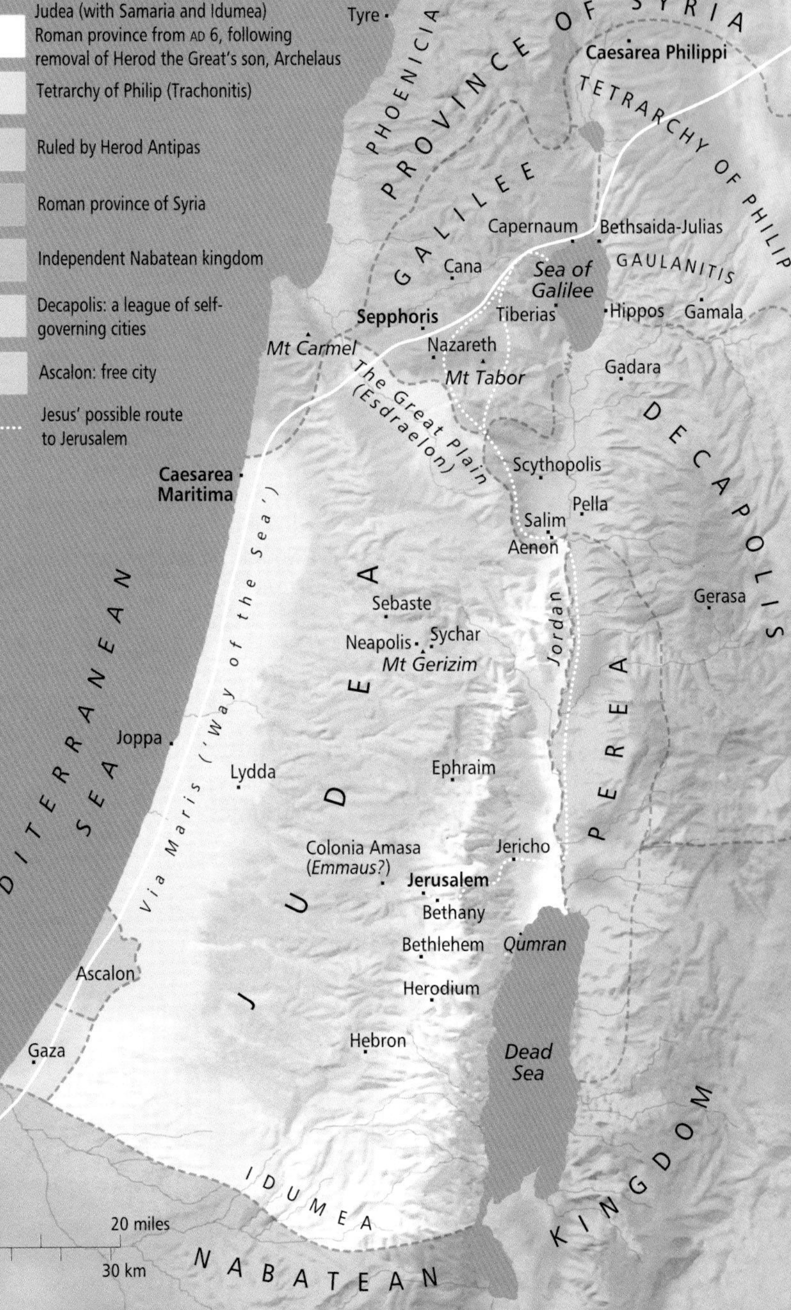

Judea (with Samaria and Idumea) Roman province from AD 6, following removal of Herod the Great's son, Archelaus
Tetrarchy of Philip (Trachonitis)
Ruled by Herod Antipas
Roman province of Syria
Independent Nabatean kingdom
Decapolis: a league of self-governing cities
Ascalon: free city
Jesus' possible route to Jerusalem
Tyre
PHOENICIA
PROVINCE OF SYRIA
Caesarea Philippi
TETRARCHY OF PHILIP
GALILEE
Capernaum
Bethsaida-Julias
Cana
Sea of Galilee
GAULANITIS
Sepphoris
Tiberias
Hippos
Gamala
Mt Carmel
Nazareth
Mt Tabor
Gadara
The Great Plain (Esdraelon)
DECAPOLIS
Caesarea Maritima
Scythopolis
Pella
Salim
Aenon
Via Maris ('Way of the Sea')
MEDITERRANEAN SEA
Sebaste
Gerasa
Neapolis
Sychar
Mt Gerizim
Jordan
JUDEA
PEREA
Joppa
Lydda
Ephraim
Colonia Amasa (Emmaus?)
Jericho
Jerusalem
Bethany
Bethlehem
Qumran
Ascalon
Herodium
Hebron
Gaza
Dead Sea
IDUMEA
NABATEAN KINGDOM
20 miles
30 km

Judaism (chapters 5–7). After that, we follow Jesus to his destiny in Jerusalem, the centre of that Jewish world. But something surprising happens there, which enables people to see 'Jesus and his world' in a new light.

This book, like many others, really has more than one author. So I am truly grateful to those who have influenced what now appears under my name: especially, friends at Wycliffe Hall, Oxford, and Christ Church, Abingdon; also Morag Reeve, Angela Handley, Jenni Dutton and Nick Rous at Lion Publishing.

To write about Jesus is a daunting task. For anyone who has tried to be a follower of this Jesus, writing such a book becomes a personal reflection on one's own spiritual journey. You keep remembering the time you first discovered the point you are now trying to convey to others. It is also a humbling task, as you hope that nothing you have written on this most important topic may cause confusion – especially if it conflicts with interpretations faithfully held for many years. And it is also a challenge: how am I responding to the great truths I keep finding in this one remarkable life?

For that reason, no book on Jesus could ever be complete – there will always be so much to say. So please treat this book as a mere taster before the real thing. And if you find yourself going back in a fresh way to the Gospels, those brilliant first 'biographies' of Jesus, then this author will be well pleased.

CHAPTER 1

The Story of Jesus

'He was born in an obscure village to parents who were peasants. Mostly he worked as a carpenter, but he became a travelling preacher…

'Two thousand years have passed, yet he still remains the figure at the very heart of the human race. All the kings, rulers and powers that have ever been, all the armies that have ever fought, indeed nothing since time began, has had so great an effect upon the course of human history as that one solitary life.'

The anonymous author who wrote these words may have been overstating the case, but not by much. The quote captures well an issue that we need to remember throughout this book: why has a prophet from a Middle Eastern village called Nazareth had such an influence on the world, seemingly out of all proportion to his few years of teaching? He never wrote a book, but 2,000 years later, not an hour will go by without his name being mentioned somewhere on the face of the planet. Of all the figures of history, he is the one about whom most books have been written.

So what was Jesus' secret? What is it about him that continues to attract such interest? Is it the sheer quality of his teaching, so simple and yet so profound? Is it the awesome sense of God's reality that he seems to have possessed and been able to pass on to others? Is it something to do with his character? Or was he perhaps just the 'right person at the right time'? Maybe Jesus, born as he was within the first 10 years of the reign of Emperor

'I have regarded Jesus of Nazareth as one among the mighty teachers that the world has had... I shall say to the Hindus that your lives will be incomplete unless you reverently study the teachings of Jesus.'

MOHANDAS K. GANDHI, *THE MESSAGE OF JESUS CHRIST*, 1938

Augustus (which gave the ancient world at long last an era of peace), knew that this was the perfect time to launch a new religious system throughout the Roman empire? Some suggest that people were increasingly disenchanted with contemporary philosophies – there was a spiritual vacuum. Certainly within Jesus' own homeland, the land of Israel, a sense of despair had set in after the return of foreign occupation in 63 BC. How could Judaism continue to see itself as containing the truth of the one true God for the whole world – let alone persuade others of this fact – if it was habitually hemmed in by pagan oppressors?

The timing was indeed important. In a sense, what Jesus achieved was to snatch up the brilliant essence of Judaism and make it available on a much wider scale. And he did so just in time – before Rome destroyed the Jewish capital of Jerusalem in AD 70.

Yet, even if the timing was ideal, the explanation for Jesus' influence ultimately comes back, as we shall see, to his own person and in particular to the pivotal events in Jerusalem at the end of his ministry. He died on a Roman cross, and that should have been the end of the story. But for some reason, which we shall attempt to discover and examine in these pages, it was not.

The lowest place on the planet: the Dead Sea, looking from the Judean desert across to the hills of Moab.

A singular life

The basic outline of Jesus' life is well known to many, but it is helpful to remind ourselves of its most important details. The New Testament is the collection of writings treasured by the first Christians: in it, there are various letters, a short history of the early church and four accounts of Jesus' life. These are known by the Anglo-Saxon word 'Gospels' because they contain 'good news': Matthew, Mark, Luke and John. If for the moment we take these at their face value, what do we know of Jesus' life? Most of the following outline is based on Mark's Gospel (especially chapters 1–8).

'"I will send my messenger ahead of you... a voice of one calling in the desert, 'Prepare the way for the Lord...'" And so John came, baptizing in the desert region.'

MARK 1:2, 3, 4

Jesus was born in Bethlehem, but spent his largely unchronicled childhood in the tiny Jewish village of Nazareth. The story of the adult Jesus, the main focus of the Gospels, commences when he is in his thirties, probably in or around the year which we now know as AD 29. His public career seems to have been launched when he travelled to a point on the River Jordan just north of the Dead Sea. His cousin John the Baptist was there summoning the people of Israel to go through a strange rite – baptism – going down into the waters of the river as a sign that they wanted to be considered clean in God's sight. It was a sign that they would be ready for that moment when God at last acted to bless his people. And Jesus was 'baptized' too.

Jesus then seems to have gone into the nearby Judean desert for a period of solitude – a time, no doubt, for prayerful reflection and for thinking more deeply about his sense of vocation. Then he returned to Galilee and started an itinerant ministry, going through villages and synagogues, teaching in God's name with great authority and performing some remarkable acts of healing. His central theme was the 'kingdom of God' – the news that Israel's God would at last be recognized as the true king.

His base of operations now shifted from Nazareth to Capernaum, a fishing village on the northern shores of Lake Galilee. It might be small but it was strategically placed on a major trade route. So it was an ideal place for a preacher to be heard by many from far and wide. For the next three years, this beautiful lake and the surrounding hills would become the scene of some extraordinary events, as the prophet from Nazareth amazed people with his teaching, his knowledge of the living God, his holiness and his compassion. He also gained a reputation for his miraculous power over nature. So we have accounts of Jesus healing the blind and the paralysed, and curing epileptics and lepers. Tales spread of him walking on water; of him bringing back to life a 12-year-old girl and a corpse in the midst of a funeral procession.

Remains of the synagogue at Capernaum; this was built some centuries after Jesus, but possibly on the site of the synagogue of Jesus' day.

It was not surprising that he began to gain quite a following. He travelled with an inner group of 12 male disciples and a large entourage of men and women who were regularly in his company. When he taught, huge numbers of people flocked to hear. On one occasion, he had to get into a boat to avoid being crushed, but continued to teach the people as they sat around a natural amphitheatre still visible in the shoreline just west of Capernaum.

Another time, over 5,000 people followed him to the deserted area on the north-eastern side of the lake and then realized it was too late to go anywhere to buy food. When Jesus was somehow able to feed them all with five loaves and two fishes, some of them tried to make this wonder-worker into their king. They wanted him to take his campaign to Jerusalem, but he slipped through the crowd and escaped.

This incident gives a good clue as to what attracted many in the crowds. This was a region – Galilee – where revolutionaries were longing for the Roman oppressors to be thrown out of the land. And now this preacher was announcing 'the kingdom of God is near'. Israel's God was about to act. This was political and religious dynamite – the time for which Jesus' contemporaries had been waiting. This incident also reveals Jesus' difficulty in getting his own message across without being misunderstood. What if God's kingdom was going to be ushered in, but not through physical force? What if Jesus was a king, but of a different kind? What if he was intending to go to Jerusalem but had a different agenda?

'Jesus went throughout Galilee, teaching in their synagogues, preaching the good news of the kingdom, and healing every disease... News about him spread all over Syria.'

MATTHEW 4:23, 24

Inevitably, Jesus also had his opponents. Although for some people his words were not revolutionary enough, for others they went much too far. Jesus' attitudes towards some traditions were not what people were expecting. Nor was the company he kept. He soon caught the eye of the religious authorities in Jerusalem – not least when he claimed to be able to forgive people their sins.

Then Jesus took his immediate followers with him on a journey into the villages surrounding Caesarea Philippi. In these isolated surroundings, where there was no danger of interruption or rushed confusion, Jesus impressed upon them his true identity and his true mission. He was the long-awaited king, the 'anointed' Messiah. And, yes, he was going up to Jerusalem for Passover, the great springtime festival that celebrated the Israelites' deliverance from

Egypt. Jesus had been to Jerusalem in previous years (for a variety of different festivals), but this time the disciples sensed it would be different. And indeed it would. Jesus went on to explain: the Messiah was going up to Jerusalem in order to die.

The rest is history. We will pick up the story of Jesus' journey to Jerusalem later and go through in more detail what the Gospels claim happened there – from his dramatic entrance to his final arrest and crucifixion. And also, of course, we shall investigate that bizarre claim, made by each of the Gospel writers, that something unique happened on the 'third day' after his death. Whatever it was, it was a surprising climax to an already fascinating story. And it will send us back, as it did Jesus' first followers, to ask: who exactly was Jesus?

'A character so original, so complete, so uniformly consistent, so perfect, so human and yet so high above human greatness, can be neither a fraud nor a fiction… It would take more than a Jesus to invent a Jesus.'

PHILIP SCHAFF, *HISTORY OF THE CHRISTIAN CHURCH*, 1888

A journey of discovery

This all seems intriguing, but what do we make of it? Told like this, it could sound like an ancient story from one particular place which, for all its interesting features, is

The life of Jesus: the annunciation

According to Luke, the remarkable story of Jesus begins at his conception. In his Gospel (perhaps relying on the memory of Jesus' mother), Luke relates that Nazareth received a strange visitor. A young girl called Miriam (or Mary) was told by an angel, a messenger of God, that, by the power of God's Spirit, she would give birth to a boy who would 'be called the Son of the Most High' (Luke 1:32). This visit was later called the annunciation.

Both Jesus and Mary would be vulnerable to vicious rumour and could be called unpleasant names – this kind of story was easily misconstrued. Even Mary's fiancé Joseph had serious doubts – until he too was addressed by God (Matthew 1:18–21). 'The virgin will be with child…' (Isaiah 7:14, quoted in Matthew 1:23).

not really very relevant for people in quite different cultures and at a vastly different point in human history. For millions, though, this is the ultimate story, the most important one of all time.

If we are going to understand this story properly, we will need, first, to understand something about its geographical setting (chapter 2). Then we will need to ask just how reliable the written sources are (chapter 3) and examine some of the various ways of interpreting them (chapter 4). We will also need to enter more deeply into the thought-world of Jesus' contemporaries (chapter 5). Only then, perhaps, will we be able to establish something of Jesus' own aims for his ministry (chapter 6) and what exactly he was challenging people to do (chapter 7). Then we will follow Jesus to Jerusalem (chapters 8–11) – to see what happens next.

The 16th-century Annunciation Tapestry in the Cathedral of Rheims, France.

CHAPTER 2

The Palestine of Jesus

Jesus lived in the Roman province of Palestina, the narrow strip of land between the desert of Trans-Jordan to the east and the Mediterranean Sea to the west. Almost exactly 1,000 years before, much of this territory had belonged to King David, the most renowned of Israel's kings, but the intervening centuries had seen the Jewish ownership of this land wax and wane. It was too important a stretch of land to be left unmolested by the world's leading powers. Assyrians, Babylonians, Egyptians and Greeks had all marched through it, and now, most recently, it had been taken over by the Romans.

The contours of the land

What was Jesus' homeland like? In terms of agriculture, it was not nearly as productive as its neighbour, Egypt (blessed with the waters of the River Nile). In the land of Jesus, there were some fertile areas but not many: chiefly the coastal plains and the plain of Jezreel (just below the hills of Nazareth, Jesus' childhood home). Otherwise the province was dominated either by inhospitable desert (in the south and east) or by the rugged terraces of the hill country (running down the spine of the country, from north to south).

To be sure, the prevailing westerly winds, which came in from the Mediterranean and met this range of hills, ensured a reasonable amount of rainfall during the six winter months. So it was known as the 'land flowing with milk and honey' (at least when compared with the Sinai desert further to the south). But the Jewish residents also told an amusing proverb about God's creation of the world which gave a slightly different impression: a stork carrying 10 baskets of rock to be distributed evenly around the world mistakenly dropped nine of them on the land of Israel! It was indeed very barren in places and full of rocks. Over the centuries many of the hillsides had been covered in stone-built terraces as farmers tried to increase the amount of fertile soil in this otherwise quite inhospitable terrain.

Terraced fields in the Judean hills.

Although the province had a long Mediterranean coastline, most of the inhabitants were fearful of the sea. In fact, there were very few natural harbours along this coast – hence the major engineering feats that were required for constructing the impressive port at Caesarea Maritima. Instead people saw themselves connected to the outside world by two significant land routes: south to Egypt and north-east to Damascus and Mesopotamia. These two routes made up the ancient Via Maris (the 'Way of the Sea'), one of the most important trade routes in the ancient world. The land of Israel thus acted as a land bridge between the continents of Asia and Africa. As a result, the

The towns of Galilee and the harbours on Lake Galilee in New Testament times.

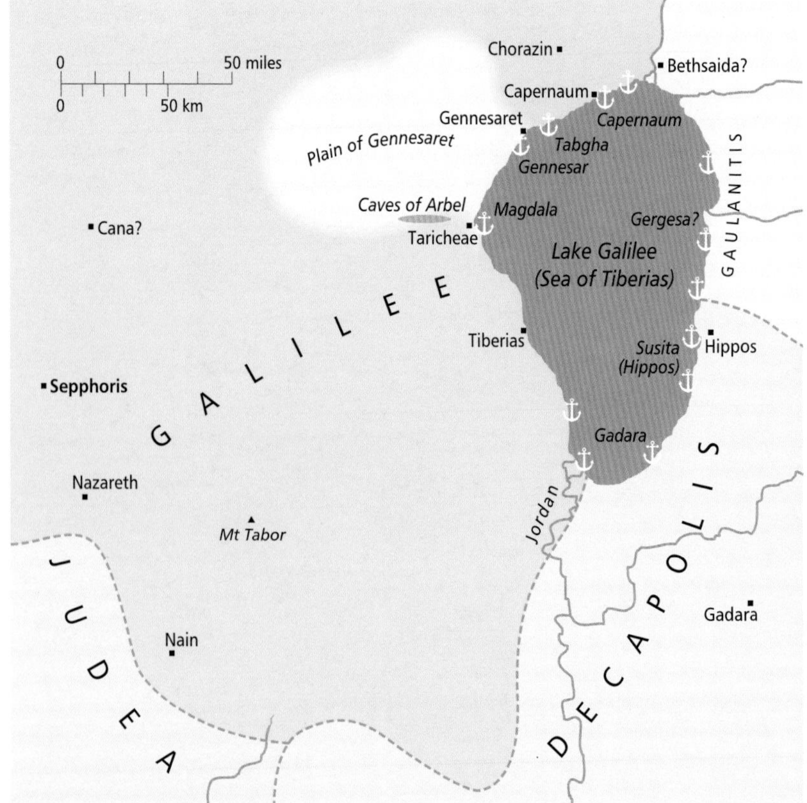

country was seldom allowed to have any lasting peace. It was always the buffer between world empires on either side.

The region of Galilee in the north lay exactly on the route between Damascus and Egypt, so it was no cultural backwater. If anything, it was Jerusalem, the main city in the province, that was in danger of being cut off from the surrounding culture – precisely because it was not on this trade route. Jerusalem could remain a more isolated, Jewish city; Galilee would always feel like it was on the frontier with the wider world.

The central feature of Galilee was its large inland lake (13 miles by 8 miles at its widest, and shaped like a harp). The lake was fed with fresh water from the snow-capped slopes of Mount Hermon just 40 miles to the north. Not surprisingly, fishing was a major industry with lots of cooperatives running small businesses. The names of some of the villages by the lake reflect this: 'Bethsaida' means 'fishing village', Tarichaeae (the alternative name for 'Magdala') has been translated as 'processed Fishville'!

The other lake in the province – the aptly named Dead Sea – was quite a contrast. None of the water entering the Dead Sea from the River Jordan could escape, except by evaporation; the water that remained was stagnant and full of chemicals. Few people, apart from a few hermits, lived in this desolate region. A few miles to the north, however, was Jericho – the oldest city in the world – located in an oasis at the head of a stunning rift valley. It was a beautiful city full of palm trees; some of Jerusalem's upper class built their winter homes here.

And then there was Jerusalem itself, perched on the crest of the Judean hills. It was only 14 miles west of Jericho, but the approach from the east involved a steep climb through desert until you reached the Mount of Olives. Once over the crest of the Mount, the traveller was greeted with a stunning view of the 'holy city'. This was Jerusalem, the 'city of peace', the central city within Jewish life.

Standing on the Mount of Olives today, one can imagine how this impressive panorama might have looked

Previous pages: View of Jerusalem's Old City from the Mount of Olives. The temple would have stood on the site now marked by the golden 'Dome of the Rock' mosque.

in Jesus' day. In the centre, beyond the Kidron valley, would have been Israel's temple, which King Herod the Great (the Idumean king who ruled Palestine from 37 BC until 4 BC) had begun rebuilding and extending some 15 years before the birth of Jesus. Further to the left were the older parts of the city, going back to the time of King David. But now the city had also spread onto another hill in the distance.

This western quarter of the city would still have been fairly visible from the Mount of Olives. It was where Herod had recently built himself a palace and where most of Jerusalem's wealthier citizens had their houses – cooled by the westerly breezes and not 'downwind' of the temple with the stench of its many sacrifices. The population of Jerusalem was normally around 120,000 and expanding year by year. For this was the city at the heart of the Jewish nation, and the place which hosted three pilgrim-festivals each year. Looking at it spread out before them from the Mount of Olives, few pilgrims coming up from Galilee could have seen it without being impressed.

A weaver at work in the 'Nazareth Village'.

The people of the land

The majority of people lived on the land. Their daily lives would have been very similar to other rural communities around the Mediterranean. Apart from the few major centres of population it was an agrarian society, with close-knit communities tied to the land for successive generations. Families and kinship groups were vitally important; farming and cottage industries were the norm. If people here were different from those elsewhere in the empire, it was because of religion. The majority of the population were Jewish and therefore quite resistant to the encroaches of Greek culture.

The Jews had a long history associated

with the land, going back more than 1,000 years. They had been devastated by two major invasions (the Assyrians in the 8th century and the Babylonians in the 6th century BC) and had rebuilt their homeland in the area around Jerusalem. Gradually they had expanded and in the 2nd century BC had even established an independent kingdom under the

A carpenter at work in the 'Nazareth Village'.

Hasmonean dynasty in the face of a possible Greek invasion. But that had come to an end with the arrival of the Roman armies under Pompey in 63 BC. Rome needed a strong buffer state on the eastern rim of its empire, so the Roman forces were unlikely to be going away in the near future. The result was an incredible resentment among the local people, finding themselves occupied by this 'superpower' from the west.

Inevitably this meant there was a significant Roman presence in the province. Latin was spoken by the soldiers and in some of the civic administration – especially in Caesarea Maritima. The Jews themselves tended to speak Aramaic (the more colloquial form of Hebrew), but they used Hebrew in their synagogues and possibly for everyday use as well. However, as in all other provinces of the Eastern Mediterranean, the lingua franca was Greek. After all, educated Romans spoke Greek themselves, and Greek would also have been the first language for the quite significant number of non-Jews who lived in the province – especially in the coastal plain and in the area known as the Decapolis (the 'Ten Cities').

These Greek cities surrounded some of Lake Galilee itself. So the Jews living in Galilee were surrounded by

The massive aqueduct built by Herod to bring water into Caesarea Maritima.

'Gentiles' (in other words, non-Jews). Moreover, the most direct route for Galileans wishing to visit Jerusalem was blocked by the central hill country inhabited by their long-term enemies, the Samaritans. Jews and Samaritans tried to avoid each other as much as possible, as each believed the other to be ritually unclean. Jews living in Galilee were, therefore, effectively cut off from Jerusalem by this large no-go area right in the middle of the country.

So it was clearly a province with various tensions bubbling away just under the surface – the conflict between Jews and Samaritans, the conflict with occupying Rome, and the ongoing conflict between rich and poor.

The province was far from wealthy, but what personal wealth there was rested firmly in the hands of the urban elite (perhaps no more than five per cent of the population). As an agrarian society, it had developed an elaborate system of patronage. This meant that the poorer 'clients' were honour-bound to their patrons, with money and goods frequently passing in a vertical direction rather than being spread among the populace. Debt was running high, farmers were being dispossessed of their ancestral landholdings, and large estates were growing up in their stead.

Caesarea Maritima

Herod the Great's new port, Caesarea Maritima, became the administrative capital of the province of Palestina. Excavations have revealed its splendour: the massive harbour walls (built using the recent invention of concrete); its aqueducts and its underground sewage system (flushed twice daily by the tides); some pagan temples (dedicated to the emperor and to the god Mithras); a hippodrome and a theatre. The contrast with Jewish Jerusalem is striking. Almost certainly, Jesus never visited the port but his message soon attracted a Roman centurion who was posted there (Acts 10–11).

Taxation, too, was very high. During his reign, Herod the Great claimed a third of all Palestinian grain and half of the fruit. From the local population, the Romans commandeered tax collectors – middlemen who collected various taxes, including transit taxes and a 'head tax' (one denarius per person per year, the equivalent of a day's wage for a labourer). The Jerusalem temple required a half-shekel tax each year, and various other 'taxes' in the form of tithes, sacrifices and vows.

Despite this economic hardship, villagers and farmers seldom came out in revolt. In the years since Jesus' birth, however, there had been a marked increase in 'social banditry' – groups of disaffiliated young men taking the law into their own hands and attacking the local estates, Roman garrisons and supply lines. Often these bandits came from Galilee which, compared with Jerusalem, was very much the 'poor relation' and a continual hotbed of unrest.

Some recent history

Fortunately for the Romans there had been some tough local management. Herod the Great, though neither Jewish nor Roman, had kept the province under an iron grip for over 30 years until his death in c. 4 BC. His reign had been marked by an elaborate building programme: founding the city of Sebaste in Samaria and Caesarea Maritima on the coast, and, above all, rebuilding Jerusalem's temple.

'Herod was evil to all alike; he easily gave in to anger and despised justice.'

JOSEPHUS, *ANTIQUITIES* 17:191

But Herod's reign had also been marked, especially in his later years, by his paranoid brutality. Countless people had been put to death, including some of his sons. In the Gospels, he is depicted ordering the massacre of innocent children in Bethlehem and this would have been quite in character. Herod had his own defence bunker just five miles to the south-east of Bethlehem on the edge of the Judean desert – an impregnable fortress to which he could flee if under attack.

After his death there was a major uprising, led by Judas the Galilean, but it was put down severely by the

The life of Jesus: his birth

Jesus' birth, so well known from Christmas celebrations, is only described in Luke 2:1–20. Luke speaks of the journey from Nazareth to Bethlehem (about five days by mule) so that Joseph could comply with a Roman census, and of Jesus being born in an animal shelter and then placed in a feeding trough (a 'manger') – 'because there was no room in the inn'.

Bethlehem (the 'house of bread') was a tiny village seven miles south of Jerusalem, the home of the great King David (c. 1000 BC) – a suitable place for the arrival of another king from humble origins. Jesus' 'royal' birth was certainly unusual.

The Shepherds Follow the Star of Bethlehem **by Octave Penguilly-L'Haridon (1811–70).**

Some homes were built out from natural caves which, because of their warmth, were then used for animals. So, Jesus' birthplace, though not ideal, may have provided some welcome warmth and privacy.

Matthew then describes what happened later – the Magi from the East, Joseph and Mary's escape to Egypt with Jesus, and Herod's massacre of all the local boys under two (Matthew 2:1–18). Herod died in 4 BC, so Jesus was probably born in 6 or 5 BC. There are various explanations of the 'star in the east', but one recent theory (of a comet known from Chinese records) suggests a date between March and May in 5 BC. Although the church later adopted 25 December as the official celebration of Jesus' birth, a springtime birth makes more sense of the shepherds sleeping out in the fields.

Roman authorities. They then divided up Herod's territory into four areas, spread between Herod's three sons: Herod Antipas ruled Galilee and Perea, Herod Philip the area to the north-east of Galilee (known as Batanaea or Gaulanitis), and Archelaus the area around Jerusalem. But after 10 years, Archelaus was ousted by the Romans who imposed direct rule on 'Judea'. So it was that various procurators took office in Caesarea and Jerusalem, the most famous of which, for reasons connected to our story, would be Pontius Pilate.

The Palestine in which Jesus grew up, then, was politically red-hot. It was not a place where a public figure could afford to put a foot wrong. Throughout his life the tension between the Jews and the Roman rulers was increasing. The political disturbances during this period culminated eventually in the Jewish Revolt against Rome in AD 66. When Jesus preached, he did so in a context that was like a tinderbox waiting to go up in flames.

With the destruction of the Jerusalem temple in AD 70, that is precisely what happened. The world that Jesus knew went up in flames and effectively disappeared off the map. Its centre lay in ruins. But by then (and just in time) Jesus had done something that moved the storyline of Israel into a whole new dimension and gave it the resources to cope with a world which no longer revolved around the temple. What Jesus had given, in fact, was a whole new centre – namely himself.

CHAPTER 3

The Evidence for Jesus

The last chapter set the context. Now it is time to examine the evidence for the life of Jesus. As with all historical figures, our knowledge of them must be gained either through archaeology or, more often, through written accounts. In the case of Jesus, it is useful to draw a further distinction between those sources written by people outside the Christian community and those penned by his followers. So we will look at each of these three areas in turn: archaeology, non-Christian sources and Christian sources.

The so-called 'Jesus boat', discovered on the shores of Lake Galilee during the drought of 1986.

Archaeological evidence

Archaeology in what is often referred to as the 'Holy Land' is a flourishing science, and anything that connects with the story of Jesus automatically has an extra appeal. Recent years have seen many discoveries: excavations in Jerusalem's Old City have revealed the wealthy houses of the 'upper city' and the area near the Temple Mount; numerous 1st-century Jewish tombs and ossuaries have been found; the Dead Sea Scrolls have been published; towns in Galilee have been excavated; and, perhaps most intriguing of all, a 1st-century boat has been recovered from the mud at the bottom of Lake Galilee (in the droughts of 1986). No wonder the Holy Land has been described by some as a 'fifth Gospel'.

But nothing that has yet been found provides direct evidence for Jesus himself. The nearest might be an ossuary box (brought to light only in 2002), labelled as having contained the bones of a 'James, brother of Jesus'. Could this be the brother of Jesus of Nazareth? Jesus himself never wrote anything. Nor has he left any archaeological evidence that can be attributed to him alone. Visitors to the Holy Land today often comment that they came to find Jesus and instead find Herod the Great. If we are looking at the era of Jesus in this land, then the stones speak volumes about Herod, very little about Jesus. Jesus walked and talked, whereas Herod built.

In this sense, archaeology reveals its limitations. It can help us to understand a written source better and provide invaluable supporting evidence. But it can rarely disprove a supposed historical event. An 'argument from silence' (lack of evidence) rarely works in the realm of archaeology.

What archaeology has done, then, during the last 150 years is throw light on the biblical narrative. It has also confirmed the general reliability of the New Testament, showing that it was far from pure invention: there was a violent ruler called Herod, who towards the end of his life lashed out against potential rivals (cf. Matthew 2:16); there were Gentiles living on the eastern shore of Lake Galilee (cf. Mark 5:1–20); there was a Roman prefect called Pontius Pilate (as proved by a Latin plaque discovered at Caesarea in 1961); there were three languages in use at that time (cf. Pilate's written charge over Jesus' cross in John 19:20); and, despite earlier scepticism, archaeologists have uncovered the pool of Bethesda with its unusual 'five porticoes' (John 5:2f.). Thus, in these five examples we

The first archaeological evidence for Pontius Pilate: an inscription found at Caesarea Maritima in 1961.

can see that archaeology confirms the general reliability of the written accounts. But it stops short of being direct evidence for Jesus himself. For that, we must turn to the written evidence.

Non-Christian sources

Jesus is referred to by both Jewish and 'pagan' sources. In the latter category, there are five of special interest (see 'Non-Christian texts', below). Coming as they do from writers who were seemingly hostile to the Christian faith, these references are a powerful corroboration of Jesus'

Non-Christian texts

Pliny the Younger, when governor of Bithynia (c. AD 112), wrote to the Emperor Trajan about Christians who refused to revere the emperor's image: 'they sang in alternate verses a hymn to Christ as to a god' (*Epistles* 10:96).

Tacitus, the Roman historian (c. AD 60–120), explained the presence of Christians in Rome, whom Nero blamed for the great fire of AD 64: 'Christus, the founder of the name, had undergone the death penalty in the reign of Tiberius, by sentence of the procurator Pontius Pilate. The pernicious superstition was checked for a moment, only to break out once more, not merely in Judea, the home of the disease, but in the capital itself, where all things horrible or shameful in the world collect and find a vogue' (*Annals* 15:44).

Suetonius, another Roman historian (c. AD 75–160) is probably referring to 'Christus', when he reports on Claudius's expulsion of the Jews from Rome in AD 49 (cf. Acts 18:2): 'since the Jews constantly made disturbances at the instigation of Chrestus, he expelled them from Rome' (*Life of Claudius* 25:4).

Mara ben Serapion, a Stoic living in the 3rd century, wrote to his son about the martyrdoms of Socrates and Christ: 'The Jews in executing their wise king were driven from the land... Nor did the wise king die for good; he lived on in the teaching which he had given' (in a 7th-century manuscript in the British Museum).

Julius Africanus (a Christian writer, c. AD 190) notes how a pagan named Thallus had discussed the darkness at Jesus' crucifixion and suggested (incorrectly) that this was a solar eclipse (*Chronology* 18).

existence and death. Two of them hint at the strange continuation of Jesus' influence after his criminal death; one notes the oddity of his being worshipped 'as a god' and one confirms what we know from the New Testament of the tensions caused within Jewish synagogues by the preaching of the name of Jesus as Messiah or 'Christ'.

It is just possible that Tacitus had access to some official records in Rome, despatched by Pontius Pilate (some 'Acts of Pilate' are referred to by Justin Martyr in AD 160). Otherwise the Roman writers only know about Jesus because of the activities of his followers in Rome. What they report may itself then be dependent on what they have heard Christians teaching. Jesus' own ministry, located in the eastern backwater of Palestine, was hardly the stuff to make the Roman headlines. All this is entirely what we would expect.

When we turn to Jewish sources, the most famous reference to Jesus comes in Josephus, the historian of the Jewish revolt. It looks most impressive, but almost certainly a Christian copyist has added some phrases to the original text (probably those in square brackets: see 'The testimony of Josephus', below). Josephus's other

The testimony of Josephus

About this time comes Jesus, a wise man [if indeed it is proper to call him a man]. For he was a worker of incredible deeds, a teacher of those who accept the truth with pleasure, and he attracted many Jews as well as many Greeks. [This man was Christ.] And when, in view of his denunciation by the leading men among us, Pilate had him sentenced to a cross, those who had loved him at the beginning did not cease. [He appeared to them on the third day alive again, for the divine prophets had announced these and countless other marvels concerning him.] And even now the tribe of the 'Christians' – named after him – has not yet disappeared.

JOSEPHUS, *ANTIQUITIES* 18:63–64, WRITING IN ROME c. AD 93

reference to Jesus is far more likely to be authentic: he describes how in AD 62 the high priest 'brought before the Sanhedrin a man named James, the brother of Jesus who was called the Christ' (*Antiquities* 20:200). Josephus knows that some of his fellow Jews thought Jesus was the Messiah and, unlike the pagan writers, Josephus may have had access to Jewish accounts of Jesus – not just the teaching of his followers. Josephus is then a powerful early and independent witness to Jesus.

There may also be a significant reference to Jesus in a later Jewish document known as the Babylonian Talmud: 'On the eve of Passover Yeshu was hanged. For 40 days beforehand, a herald cried: "He is to be stoned because he has practised sorcery and enticed Israel to apostasy..."' (Sanhedrin 43a). This agrees with the Gospel account of Jesus' death at Passover time and his being accused of leading Israel astray (see Matthew 27:63); it also confirms that, although the normal punishment for apostasy was stoning, Jesus was 'hanged' (that is, crucified). Note, too, how no attempt is made to suggest Jesus died simply because of the Romans.

But we cannot be sure that such a text goes back to any eyewitnesses. The Talmud is a collection of sayings finally put together around AD 500 and, although it drew on the much older Mishnah, much of this present section may be the result of later debates – as Jews rebutted the Christians' claims. The Jewish sources are thus important: they confirm Jesus' existence and hint at his significance. But they do not offer material that a historian could safely use in reconstructing the life of Jesus himself.

'Jesus did many other things as well. If every one of them were written down... the whole world would not have room for the books that would be written.'

JOHN 21:25

Christian sources outside the Bible

It has long been recognized that not everything that Jesus did has necessarily been preserved in the four Gospels as found in the Bible. The writer of John's Gospel acknowledges his own selectivity (John 21:25) and early Christians such as Papias (C. AD 130) liked to supplement the written record, if they could, with any oral tradition which might go back to the apostles. Later Christian writings record some 20 short sayings that might possibly go back to Jesus (the so-called 'agrapha').

At this point, however, we have to recognize that, during the 2nd century in particular, there were numerous books written by splinter Christian groups, many of which were claiming to go back to the apostles (Gospel of Thomas, Gospel of Peter, Gospel of Barnabas, etc.). Most of these so-called 'apocryphal Gospels' are recognized as containing very little that is authentic. The Gospel of Peter, for example, heavily embellishes the story of the crucifixion and resurrection. There are also two works which try to fill out the childhood years of Jesus (the ProtoEvangelium of James and the Infancy Gospel of Thomas). Yet few people give these accounts any historical weight.

The exception is the Gospel of Thomas. This text (which must be distinguished from the Infancy Gospel) was discovered as a Coptic manuscript in Egypt in 1945 and is generally dated to c. AD 150. It is a collection of 114 sayings with very little narrative structure. Many of these sayings are bizarre and some clearly reflect the influence of what is called 'gnosticism'. (This was an esoteric Christian heresy focusing on mystical inner 'knowledge' and escape from the evil of the material world; hence it tended to avoid talking about historical events such as Jesus' crucifixion.) Nevertheless, some of the sayings are close to what we find in the Gospels and are therefore independent confirmation of Jesus' words. Despite the recent work of some scholars, who try to date Thomas to the middle of the 1st century, the consensus view is that it is to be dated 100 years later and cannot be relied on for evidence about Jesus.

There are also, finally, three documents whose existence has been hypothesized by some scholars: 'Q' (a collection of Jesus' sayings, known independently to both Luke and Matthew); a Cross Gospel (from the Gospel of Peter, but perhaps preceding our Gospels); and a Secret Gospel of Mark (an earlier version of Mark). Hardly anyone, however, suggests these 'documents' can give us any reliable testimony to Jesus – in fact many scholars doubt whether they ever existed.

The four Gospels

So the Christian sources outside the Bible provide very little that can be confidently used as independent tradition concerning Jesus of Nazareth. We are left with the four accounts of Jesus' life as recorded in the New Testament – Matthew, Mark, Luke and John. These are known as the 'canonical Gospels'. 'Canonical' means they have been judged from the mid-2nd century to be within the 'canon' or 'measuring rule' of New Testament belief. John's Gospel has some distinctive emphases, but the first three present their material in quite similar terms; they are therefore known as the 'Synoptic' Gospels (because they look 'together' at Jesus, or in a similar way).

The question is: how reliable are these accounts? Just because they made it into the Bible does not mean that they are above suspicion. Can we use them to build up a reasonably historical portrait of Jesus? Endless ink, of course, has been spilt over this question – precisely because the stakes are so high. The Gospels have been subjected to a level of critical analysis that is way beyond anything inflicted on other ancient documents. And yet, after all this, a strong case can be made for saying that they basically 'told it like it was'. The criticisms levelled at the Gospels can be boiled down to four basic questions.

Are the texts reliable?

Have the texts been corrupted in transmission during the last 2,000 years? Perhaps what was originally written has not survived? After all, they were producing handwritten manuscripts that were copied by hand.

In contrast to many other ancient documents, the sheer number of surviving manuscripts for the Gospels is staggering. We mentioned above the Roman historian, Tacitus. His two books (the *Histories* and the *Annals*) have come down to us in just two manuscripts (one from the

9th century and one from the 11th century). Quite a few sections are entirely missing and at no point do these two manuscripts overlap. So, if people want to know what Tacitus wrote, they are dependent on only one manuscript – dating from nearly 1,000 years after his time. However, few classical historians have any qualms in confidently accepting the text as Tacitus's own words.

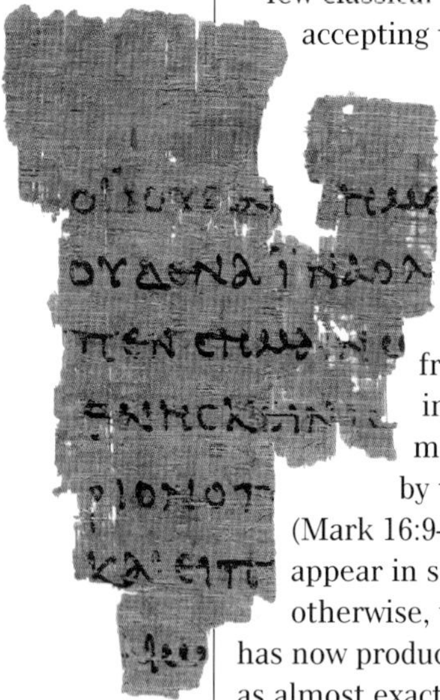

By contrast, literally thousands of handwritten copies of the Gospels in Greek have survived, some from as early as the 4th century. There are also substantial fragments going back even earlier. In fact, the earliest one is dated to no later than AD 125 – just two generations from the original 'autograph'! There are indeed some variant readings, but no major piece of the Gospel record is affected by these. There are two longer passages (Mark 16:9–20 and John 7:53 – 8:11) that do not appear in some of the early manuscripts, but otherwise, the detailed science of textual criticism has now produced a text that can be confidently received as almost exactly what the authors originally wrote.

Fragment of the oldest part of John's Gospel from c. AD 125.

Are the records sufficiently early?

Were the Gospels written too long after the event to be reliable? After all, 30 years is a long time, giving ample scope either for muddled memories or even deliberate embellishment.

Not surprisingly, then, there have been scholars who have tried to date the Gospels well into the 2nd century. But nowadays you will find few who date Mark later than 65; Matthew and Luke are often put in the 80s and John in the 90s. Personally I have argued elsewhere for Matthew being in the early 70s and Luke in the early 60s. But there are other reputable scholars who would put Matthew before 70; and in the 1980s, an otherwise quite radical scholar, John Robinson, shocked everyone by arguing with great cogency that John came first. This would mean all the Gospels were written 'within living memory'.

During much of the 20th century, it was presumed that the canonical Gospels must have been the first accounts ever to be written down. If so, then before the Gospel writers set to work the story of Jesus would have been passed on entirely by word of mouth – by 'oral tradition'. To our modern ears, that immediately conjures up notions of 'Chinese whispers' and plenty of mistakes.

In fact, however, good arguments have been made for the powerful continuity and reliability of oral tradition in non-book cultures. Homer's massive *Iliad* and *Odyssey* were often known by heart; the collection of the Buddha's sayings (the *Tripitaka*) was not written down for 400 years. Jewish Rabbis often taught their pupils by rote, and Arabic culture to this day shows the power of communities to preserve the essentials of a story through many generations. We in the modern West may not be able to remember much without the aid of scripts, but we cannot presume this was true in the time of Jesus – when books were so much rarer.

Even so, a growing minority of scholars now wonder if there were in fact some earlier accounts written before the surviving four Gospels. Some who believe in 'Q' suggest it was a written collection of Jesus' sayings. Luke himself acknowledges in his preface (1:1–3) the existence of such earlier written accounts. These are normally presumed to be Mark and Matthew, but Luke could be referring to non-canonical writings. At the very least, he is assuring his patron Theophilus that the account which follows will match up pretty closely to the tradition that Theophilus has already received in his previous Christian instruction. Some scholars in modern Jerusalem, who argue that Luke was the first Gospel, posit a Hebrew life of Jesus written in the 40s and then a Greek version in the 50s. The gap is beginning to close.

Sometimes, too, in this debate the impression is given that the apostles were not that interested in preserving

'As a literary historian I am perfectly convinced that whatever the Gospels are, they are not legends. They are not artistic enough to be legends. Most of the life of Jesus is unknown to us, and no people building up a legend would allow that to be so.'

C.S. LEWIS, *GOD IN THE DOCK*, 1952

the words of Jesus. They were too busy making history, not writing it. Or perhaps they were so convinced of Jesus' imminent return, that they did not bother to write things down – until, that is, some of them began to die, when the survivors then panicked. Some even suggest that they had a rather 'laid-back' approach, believing that their own prophetic abilities could adequately supplement the teaching of Jesus.

But at this point we have to reckon with their claim that Jesus was raised from the dead. Of course, if Jesus had been a crucified failure, then they would have had good reason for forgetting him – or else for trying to polish up his reputation by adding a few bits of their own! But if instead, as they unanimously assert, Jesus had been raised from the dead, the picture changes. As soon as they were convinced that Jesus was unique, then they would have had the highest incentive to preserve every word that had proceeded from the mouth of someone they had come to view as divine. How could they possibly dare to add to the words of the Lord? Put the resurrection in the centre of the picture and suddenly the pieces begin to fall into place.

'As a translator I felt rather like an electrician rewiring an ancient house without being able to turn the mains off.'

J.B. PHILLIPS, *LETTERS TO YOUNG CHURCHES*, 1947

Moreover, these Christians were meeting at least every Sunday to instruct one another. Indeed recent studies have shown that the apostle Paul in his letters, far from being disinterested in Jesus' life, is instead assuming that his hearers know all this already. The story of Jesus was not something trivial; it was the lifeblood of this beleaguered minority and their survival was bound up with its survival. So the Gospels are not, we suggest, a 'hit and miss' affair; nor are they woefully unreliable. They are the publication, painstakingly produced, of a much-treasured possession.

Aren't the authors biased?

A third objection recognizes that the Gospel writers (or evangelists) were indeed thoroughly committed to the cause of Jesus. Could this mean they were hopelessly biased? Wouldn't we be better off with sources that were a bit more dispassionate?

Several criticisms of the Gospels have this basic form: Christians cannot truly speak of Christ; or, convinced theologians cannot be truthful historians. But, in any other walk of life, we readily acknowledge that it is those who are most interested in their subject matter who best present it to others. The recognition of a historian's personal interests is not normally taken as an automatic reason for presuming his or her 'facts' are unreliable. Does preaching a message about a historical person require you to misrepresent the facts?

Eleventh-century mosaic of Luke the evangelist, from Hosios Lukas monastery, Greece.

The evangelists' evident commitment to the truth of their story cannot be used to discredit their accounts. Luke, for example, saw no contradiction in pursuing historical enquiry and conveying theological truth (Luke 1:1–4). The very subject matter they were describing was all about 'truth'. When you are dealing with God, truth can never be detached and merely 'objective'; it demands to be subjectively real as well. The evangelists can be both truthful and committed to that truth at the same time.

Do the four accounts agree?

Much is often made of the apparent differences between the four Gospels. John's account has a different 'feel' to it, and the three Synoptics have different emphases and some seeming clashes of detail.

This is a mammoth field and we can only make a few brief comments. First, we should get all this in a proper perspective. Classical historians would be delighted to have no fewer than four early accounts of their subject matter! Secondly, a difference in emphasis is not the same as a discrepancy. After all, witnesses at identical events pick up on different aspects. This process would naturally have affected the way the events in Jesus' life were passed on in the tradition and also the way the individual evangelists chose to write them up. It is also vital to remember that an author's selectivity is not necessarily the same thing as 'invention' or 'fabrication'.

Then again, it is presumed that two different accounts of Jesus' teaching must be a variant going back to only one original utterance. But the chances are that an itinerant preacher such as Jesus used his good one-liners more than once, and sometimes even adapted his best stories to make slightly different points. Jesus' entire teaching as recorded in Matthew's Gospel could be preached in under two hours, but one rather suspects that in three years Jesus taught for a little longer than that.

Something similar may be true of some events in Jesus' life (for example, repeated healings which were broadly similar but slightly different). And when events do seem to be recounted differently, it is not unreasonable to see if the accounts can be harmonized. Some harmonizations are ludicrous, but good historians always try to harmonize

***The life of Jesus*: his childhood**

Despite some bizarre stories in the 'apocryphal' Gospels, nothing can be reliably known of Jesus' childhood – apart from the story of his visit to Jerusalem with Mary and Joseph at the age of 12 (Luke 2:41–52).

The family would have continued living in the tiny village of Nazareth. Joseph was a 'carpenter' or even a 'stonemason' (Mark 6:3); quite possibly he was employed in the rebuilding of Sepphoris (just four miles away), the capital city of Herod Antipas, the ruler of Galilee.

Almost certainly Joseph died before the start of Jesus' ministry, but a straightforward reading of Mark 6:3 suggests Jesus had several younger brothers and sisters; initially they were sceptical about their older brother (Mark 3:21), but later James at least changed his mind (James 2:1).

different accounts first before concluding that one of them must be in error. Differences can be complementary, not contradictory.

Finally, there are occasions when insufficient notice is taken of the literary conventions of those days. The evangelists are chided with placing events in different orders when often they are working with a looser approach, more akin to an anthology selected according to themes. Or it is forgotten that Jesus spoke in Aramaic. This means that the evangelists never imagined their Greek version to convey the exact words of Jesus, but rather what is known as the 'dynamic equivalent'.

The above points will not, of course, cover every eventuality or satisfy every honest enquirer, but they may be enough to call a halt to the steady stream of people who think the differences between the Gospels automatically suggest their unreliability. In fact, for many, the existence of some of these apparent discrepancies only confirms their belief in the underlying reliability of

Christ in the House of His Parents by John Everett Millais (1829–96).

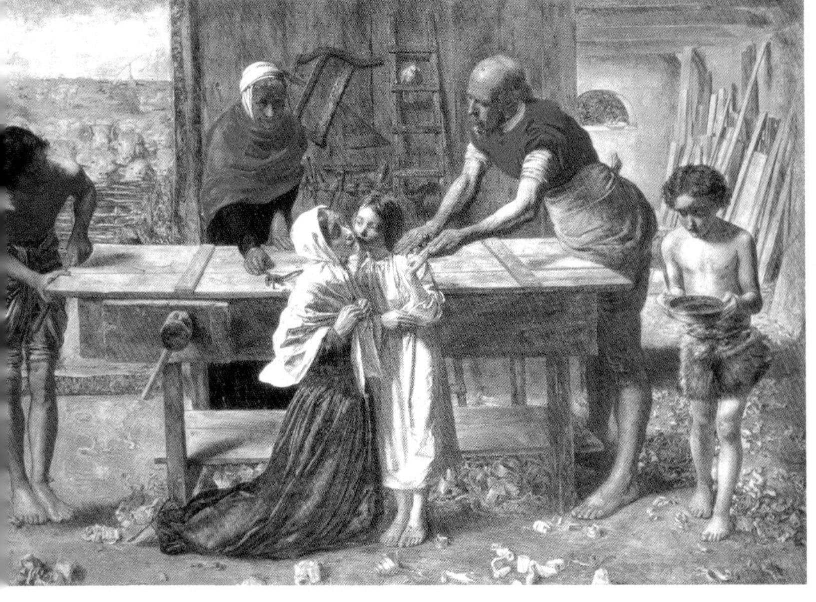

the overall picture. After all, if every account were identical, the opposite charge would readily be made – that either someone was 'cribbing' or else they were all presenting an agreed 'party line'.

Many instead rejoice in the different colours of the four Gospels: Mark, the Gospel for the individual, presenting in dramatic form the claims of Jesus the Suffering Servant; Matthew, written within and for the Jewish nation, showing Jesus as the fulfilment of Israel's hopes; Luke, written for Gentiles, portraying the human Jesus with a heart for all people; John, the Gospel for the whole world, speaking of Jesus as God incarnate within his world.

So we have looked at the different sources for our knowledge of Jesus. Written sources outside the Gospels prove his existence and death, but otherwise are disappointing. Archaeology can confirm the general background of the story but is inevitably silent about the important details. Our knowledge of Jesus turns out to be dependent on the four canonical Gospels. It has been argued here that they can bear this weight and stand up well to scrutiny: they were written quite soon after the event, by people passionate for truth. So anyone investigating the life of Jesus would do well to approach the Gospels with the assumption that they are essentially reliable and give us an account which takes us back with a sureness of touch to the Jesus of history.

CHAPTER 4

Interpreting Jesus

How do we interpret the Gospels? What is the portrait of Jesus that begins to emerge? We will begin by noting the way Jesus was represented by his first followers. We will then go on to examine the various portraits of Jesus that have emerged in scholarly circles in the last 200 years. Some of these modern approaches will be based, of course, on a far more radical approach to the reliability of the Gospels than we are proposing here. The two issues – the nature of the Gospels and the identity of Jesus – are inevitably entwined.

'It's not the parts of the Bible I don't understand that bother me; it's the parts I do understand!'

MARK TWAIN

The New Testament portrait

The New Testament writers were convinced of divine activity. For them, God had acted uniquely in the world through Jesus – 'God was in Christ' (2 Corinthians 5:19). They then came up with a variety of ways of describing who Jesus was and what he had done.

From their descriptions of Jesus, we gain an idea of how they, the people closest to Jesus, interpreted this figure from Nazareth: Jesus was the true Messiah–king of Israel, who had fulfilled the destiny of Israel to be 'a light to the nations'; he was to be identified with the 'suffering servant' promised by Isaiah, who had died for the sins of the 'many', and the 'Son of man' spoken of by the prophet Daniel; he was a prophet sent by God to speak the word of the Lord; yet at the same time he was something far greater than the prophets known in the Old Testament (such as Moses, David, and Elijah); and he was the 'Son of God', someone who called God 'Father'. Finally, although Jesus' followers were Jews and worshipped but 'one Lord', they had no hesitation in worshipping Jesus as 'Lord'. They declared that he shared a place within the divine identity.

He was the Wisdom of God, the Word of God, the presence of God, the Lamb of God. And so the list could go on. The first Christians could hardly stop themselves as they searched for words to explain the identity of Jesus. It was an explosive response and also a remarkably rapid one.

Furthermore, the early Christians very soon concluded that Jesus had possessed these identities before he arrived on the human scene. Jesus did not acquire this exalted status at some point towards the end of his ministry. Rather, he had enjoyed it for all eternity. So the coming of Jesus was an act of divine 'incarnation', a time when God himself entered into our neighbourhood and for a while took up residence in human form. This was none other than a one-off divine 'visitation'. Suddenly we are thrust into a whole new world of thought. All too soon we have left behind those quiet, uncomplicated hills of Galilee. We thought we were dealing with a story from a backwater province in the ancient world, but now we find ourselves launched into the heady realm of theology and of matters relating to eternity.

Taking in all the evidence

Focusing in this way on the whole New Testament witness, not just the Gospels, may help us to realize what we are dealing with here. The stakes are indeed high. Only once we see this clearly will we ever understand why people have tried to come up with alternative interpretations.

It also helps us to see the importance of interpreting the Gospels in the light of this wider New Testament evidence. So often in critical study of the Gospels, the other New Testament writings are conveniently left to one side. The focus is exclusively on the Gospels themselves, with interpreters thinking they have adequately finished their task when they have got behind the evangelists and uncovered their own supposedly 'original' Jesus. But good historians know they have to explain all the facts. And the fact remains that many of the New Testament letters were published within 25 years of Jesus' death – that is, before some of the Gospels themselves. They are therefore our earliest witnesses to the identity and mission of Jesus. As such, they cannot be left conveniently to one side but instead must themselves be explained.

Most importantly, we need to come up with an interpretation of Jesus of Nazareth that will adequately explain why within 20 years of his departure people were worshipping him as 'Lord' – 'Jesus is Lord' is the oldest Christian creed (see 1 Corinthians 12:3). We also need to explain the historical fact that a quite new phenomenon, the Christian church, emerged in that 1st century and spread throughout far-flung parts of the Roman empire.

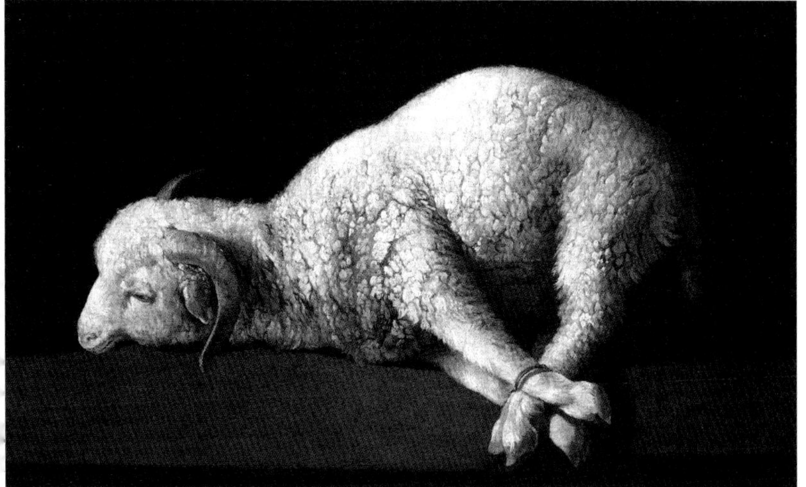

When John the Baptist saw Jesus, he proclaimed him as the 'Lamb of God, who takes away the sin of the world'. *Agnus Dei (Lamb of God)* by Francisco de Zurbaran (1598–1664).

So as historians we have to ask questions not just about the Gospels but also, for example, why the name 'Christ' was causing riots in Rome of all places in AD 49 – just over 15 years after this Messiah-figure was put to death on a Roman cross in Jerusalem. This is all part of the Jesus-phenomenon that historians have to explain.

The 'traditional' interpretation is able to make sense of this development by acknowledging one important truth: the reality of Jesus' resurrection from the dead. Once that cornerstone is in place, a reasonably straightforward linear pattern emerges: from Jesus' ministry as Messiah, through his cross and resurrection, to his being worshipped as Messiah and Lord. Take away that cornerstone, however, and immediately the story of what came next becomes almost incomprehensible. For that matter, take away the resurrection and the story of what preceded it (the ministry of Jesus) also begins to look pretty odd.

Some dangers

Yet this 'traditional' interpretation is not without its dangers. Jesus can become almost non-human, detached from the live issues of his day. He floats through in a kind of spiritual haze, intent only upon his eternal destiny, leaving only enigmatic hints as to his real purpose. And, not being truly grounded in history, this 'spiritual' Jesus can then begin to be fashioned in our own image.

This was certainly the tendency in the Gnostic and Docetic movements, both of which tried to deny the humanity of Jesus. The fact that they cropped up so soon in the church's life (well before the end of the 1st century) is, of course, tacit witness to the fact that orthodox Christians must already have been worshipping Jesus as divine. But the mainstream Christian church has often itself come close to denying Jesus' full humanity.

It was hardly surprising then that in the 18th century, a mammoth reaction set in against this sometimes impersonal Christ of church dogma, this 'Christ of faith'. Instead, the quest began to find a more historical Jesus – one less encumbered by the spiritual accretions of the church.

It is tempting for those who hold a more traditional perspective to dismiss this historical quest as unimportant. But the traditional interpretation is nothing once it loses its claim to be historical. The right response is not to abandon history, but rather to do history properly – that is, accepting the possibility of God's activity in his own world.

In this sense, 'history' can become the friend of faith. More often, however, the word is used to mean the secular interpretation of past events according to 'rational' explanations. Anything that cannot be thus explained is deemed beyond the remit of 'history'. Once we become aware of this, however, we soon realize that the traditional Jesus, even if he was the real Jesus of real history, would never be discovered using such 'historical' methods. The 'Jesus of the historians' would turn out to be only a pale shadow of the Jesus of real history.

The quest for the historical Jesus

We need to bear these points in mind as we come now to note some of the alternative interpretations of Jesus in the last 200 years. These portraits are often fruitful and always pose important questions for those who are genuinely concerned with the real Jesus.

The objection to the traditional view was launched in the 1770s by a German called Hermann Reimarus. This was the era of deism (the belief that God, if he exists, is really an absentee landlord, unable to get involved in his creation or in human affairs); it was also the age of rationalism (the assertion that reason is supreme and everything must be tested for its apparent 'reasonableness'). Working within this worldview, Reimarus went to the Gospels and advocated that the original Jesus had performed no miracles, was never raised from the dead, and did not see his death as the means of securing forgiveness.

To this day these have continued to be the frequent results of such 'historical' approaches. Other parts of the traditional portrait that frequently disappear include: Jesus' belief in his own Messiahship and his special relationship with God; his capacity to prophesy the future with regard to the fate of Jerusalem or his own 'return'; his predictions of his own death, actively intending to give up his life as some kind of sacrifice; and, of course, his virgin birth. None of this is particularly surprising if we are committed to following the modern 'gods' of deism and rationalism.

Since Reimarus, there has been a steady stream of such portraits of Jesus. In the 19th century, a man called Heinrich Paulus explained away the miracles with naturalistic explanations; David Strauss did the same using the category of myth; and Ernst Renan produced an important, but rather sentimental, depiction of Jesus in his *Life of Jesus* (1863).

In 1910, however, Albert Schweitzer published his *Quest for the Historical Jesus*. This brought these liberal lives of Jesus to an end in two important ways. First, he showed how all these reconstructions were very subjective, producing a Jesus remarkably similar to each successive historian's outlook. If we have sensed that orthodox Christians can sometimes be guilty of making Jesus in their own image, evidently the same was proving true of the historical critic.

Secondly, and more importantly, he argued that in fact the real Jesus was quite alien to modern thought because he was a Jewish apocalyptic prophet who predicted the imminent end of the world. Throughout much of the 19th century and well into the 20th century, there was an unnerving tendency for scholars to try and rescue Jesus from his Jewishness. Although his presentation of Jesus' apocalyptic tendencies went too far, Schweitzer had hit upon something vital: Jesus' essential Jewishness could not, and should not, be forgotten.

Fresco of a Jewish menorah (seven-branched candlestick), located in the Jewish catacombs in Rome, from between the 1st and 3rd centuries AD.

The result was devastating. For nearly 50 years, the quest for the historical Jesus was discontinued, with both orthodox Christians such as C.S. Lewis and radicals like Rudolph Bultmann being united in their conviction that the quest was both impossible and unnecessary. Then in the 1950s, a 'New Quest' was launched. Since the 1980s, there has been a steady stream of different approaches to the historical Jesus (see 'Jesus as portrayed by modern scholars', page 51), some associated with the American 'Jesus Seminar', some associated with the so-called 'Third Quest'.

In all such quests for the historical Jesus, the Gospels themselves are put under the closest scrutiny. In chapter 3, some arguments were given for their general reliability, but the frequent strategy in this quest is quite the opposite. The text is presumed 'suspect' until proven otherwise – even though no other ancient text is treated in this way. This has led to the development of a distinctive set of criteria for determining whether individual Gospel statements are authentic or not (for example, the criteria of 'multiple attestation', of 'dissimilarity', of 'coherence'). The results can be nit-picking and depressing.

Hence the attraction of the quite different approach espoused in recent years by N.T. Wright. He argues that normally historians work from a process of hypothesis and verification. In other words, they try to build up a

Jesus as portrayed by modern scholars

The wandering philosopher (Mack, Downing, the Jesus Seminar): Jesus was like the Cynic philosophers, helping the lower classes to be freed from social conventions.

The social prophet (Horsley): Jesus spoke out against urban elites, promoting a social revolution of peace and justice in the here and now.

The radical liberationist (Segundo, Brandon): Jesus urged more radical and even violent steps to overthrow the wealthy or the Romans.

The charismatic Jew (Vermes): Jesus was just one of several Jewish holy men ('hasidim') with miraculous powers.

The sage (Witherington): Jesus brought to life Israel's Wisdom traditions, perhaps seeing himself as embodying the personification of Wisdom.

The eschatological prophet (Meyer and 'Third Questers' such as Theissen, Sanders and N.T. Wright): Jesus was a prophet announcing a new era within God's purposes towards Israel.

plausible historical scenario and then see how much of the written material can be made to fit this reconstruction. When he does this, his results are impressive. In general, this approach blends well with an approach that allows for the different emphases and interests of the four Gospels, while affirming that they are speaking of a unified subject.

In addition to the viewpoints outlined in 'Modern portraits of Jesus' (page 51), there are, of course, some wild and maverick suggestions that come up from time to time. And a scholar like Marcus Borg is able to present a

***The life of Jesus*: his baptism**

A voice of one crying in the desert, 'Prepare the way for the Lord; make straight in the wilderness a highway for our God!'

ISAIAH 40:3; MARK 1:3

Jesus' public ministry begins with an early encounter with his cousin, John the Baptist (Luke 3). Inspired by Isaiah's words, John was calling Israel to national renewal: God was about to reveal himself and to re-form his people in judgment and restoration. Baptism was a sign of repentance and readiness; because it was more often a ritual for newcomers to Judaism, John was effectively calling his fellow Jews to start all over again.

And then Jesus came. John recognized him immediately: 'After me will come one more powerful than I… who will baptize you with the Holy Spirit.' Jesus, identifying with the sins of his own people Israel, was himself baptized. Then, 'as Jesus was coming up out of the water, he saw heaven opened and the Spirit descending on him like a dove. A voice came from heaven: "You are my Son, whom I love; with you I am well pleased!"'

The tiny River Jordan, meandering from Galilee to the Dead Sea, where Jesus was baptized by his cousin, John the Baptist.

picture of Jesus that integrates many of these strands. But some of these approaches are clearly incompatible.

Perhaps the greatest division between them resides in the issue of location/emphasis: does the historian locate Jesus primarily within a Jewish context or a non-Jewish one? Of these six approaches the first three tend to favour the latter approach: in other words, they try to find parallels to Jesus and to locate him in the setting of the ancient world in general – not primarily within Judaism. But, even if everything else is uncertain, of this we can be sure: Jesus was Jewish. Schweitzer's argument holds good.

Baptism of Christ (1416) by Jacopo and Lorenzo Salimbene, in the Oratory of St John, Urbino.

Jesus' Jewishness was not something that was merely incidental; it was the core of his being and the centre of his worldview. This is the conviction of those in the 'Third Quest'. As a result, it is they who have produced the most credible portraits of the historical Jesus and his aims.

So, in our own quest to find Jesus in his world, the time has finally come when we must narrow our search down onto that all-important inner world in which Jesus lived: not just the ancient world of the Roman province of Palestine, but the stormy, theologically charged world of Israel.

CHAPTER 5

Jesus the Jew

Judaism at the time of Jesus was a world within a world. In many ways, Judaism was 'in a world of its own', but, whether it liked it or not, it was forced (by geography and history) to interact with the wider world. And it contained within it this strange sense of vocation: Israel was to be the 'light for the world'. Somehow Israel's story was understood to be the true story of the world, the place where the God of the whole earth was peculiarly at work to bring about his purposes for the world.

It is only when we place Jesus squarely in this Jewish world, and connect him up with this longer story, that his own brief story begins to make sense. We find, too, that this works in reverse: the story of Jesus begins to make sense of the unresolved storyline of Israel. Hence it is well worth the effort to focus on Jesus' Jewishness and to see him as a real figure wrestling with the live issues of his contemporaries within Israel.

First-century Judaism

So what was it like to be a 1st-century Jew living in the 'promised land', the land promised by God to his people? Perhaps the simplest way for us to get inside the minds of Jesus and his contemporaries is to imagine them asking themselves four important questions: 'Who is our God?'; 'Who are we?'; 'What has God given us?'; and 'What is God going to do?' Each of us has a 'worldview', a mental framework which shapes our view of the world and our place in it. Worldviews are frequently revealed by our instinctive answers to significant questions ('Who am I?'; 'Where do I fit in?'; 'Where am I going?'). The four questions chosen here seem the most appropriate for 1st-century Jews, because of their religious and communal approach to life. For them, the questions were very much to do with 'God' and 'us' (not just 'me').

Who is our God?

For Jesus' contemporaries, the answer to this question was reasonably clear and uncontroversial: the God of Israel was the one true God, the creator and sustainer of the world.

'Hear, O Israel: The Lord our God, the Lord is one. Love the Lord your God with all your heart and with all your soul and with all your strength.'

THE *SHEMA*, DEUTERONOMY 6:4–5

The Hebrew scriptures taught them to believe that their God was the only God. Each day, a devout Jew would recite the *Shema* (meaning 'hear') – words from Deuteronomy that focused on the uniqueness of the Jewish God. Single-mindedness, as it were, mirrored the essential 'singleness' of God. Jews were thus ardent monotheists – believers in one God.

To many of us now, this seems comparatively unremarkable, but at that time it was quite extraordinary. It set the nation of Israel in sharp contrast to the surrounding nations, all of which were polytheistic (that is, believing in 'many gods'). No compromise was possible. The Jews were opposed to anything that might suggest that their god was just one among many, or that perhaps he could be identified with the chief god in other systems (such as Zeus or Jupiter). These other 'gods' were no gods at all; they were idols created by people.

This hard-line approach was rooted in the fact that they believed in a God of creation and providence. Taking their cue from the creation narrative in Genesis, they believed their God had created the whole world and all its people; this meant everyone should worship him alone. This then ruled out many of the views held by those in the non-Jewish world: henotheism (the belief that each nation might worship its own god); pantheism (where 'god' is simply identified with the natural order); or paganism (the view that there are many gods, often competing with one another and sometimes identified with the sun and moon, etc.). The true God was one God, separate from his creation. But he was also involved with his creation. Unlike the Epicureans (a Greek sect), the Jews believed in God's active providence: he reigned over the affairs of Israel and all the nations.

First-century Jews would also have been able to describe the character of their God. In the scriptures, he had disclosed both his nature and his special name – 'Yahweh' (meaning something like, 'I am who I am'). This God was majestic in his holiness, totally opposed to evil, yet a God of mercy and compassion. He was a God who spoke and had revealed himself to his servants and the prophets. He was a God of faithfulness, keeping his promises.

'Yahweh, the compassionate and gracious God, slow to anger, abounding in love and faithfulness, maintaining love to thousands, and forgiving wickedness, rebellion and sin. Yet he does not leave the guilty unpunished.'

EXODUS 34:6–7

But how do you explain the existence of evil within this world? This leads on to the second question.

Who are we?

First-century Jews believed that one of God's major strategies in combating evil in the world was his choice of his people, Israel. This is known as 'election' – the belief that the Jews were chosen by the living God to be his people. God then made some significant covenants (or agreements) with Israel to confirm their chosen status.

Our modern reactions to people convinced that they are the 'chosen ones' may need to be set aside for a moment. In the case of Israel, there was a very strong teaching that this election was somehow for the blessing of others. God's calling of 'Abraham and his seed' (the ancestor of the Jews and his descendants) was a divine response to the problem of human sinfulness and would in due course be for the 'blessing of many nations' (Genesis 12:1–3). In the biblical account, human sin had entered the world through the disobedience of Adam and Eve in the Garden of Eden (Genesis 2–3). Abraham was then called by God precisely in order to undo the sin of Adam, which had left humanity under God's judgment. This universal intention behind God's particular election of Israel might of course sometimes be forgotten for a

while, but it was reiterated time and time again in the Hebrew scriptures. And in Deuteronomy it is spelt out in no uncertain terms that God's choice of Israel has nothing to do with what is deserved, but everything to do with God's undeserved love (Deuteronomy 7:7–8).

Previous pages: **Israel's faith was forged in the wilderness. View from Mount Sinai at dawn.**

Jesus' Jewish contemporaries would thus have seen themselves as God's chosen people. They had a responsibility to withstand evil and to preserve the 'boundary lines' around God's people. Sometimes this opposition to the 'nations' (the Gentiles) would boil over into a vindictive spirit, looking for God's judgment on the pagans. But deep down there was an awareness that God somehow would use Israel to be a 'light to the nations'. God would use them to overcome the evil in the world.

What has God given us?

In order that Israel might withstand evil, God had also given Israel various things that were to inform and colour her whole life. These were also part of what it meant to be God's chosen people. The most important of these was the Law or Torah (which means 'instruction'). God's commandments were to be seen as a gracious gift to the people whom he had graciously chosen. Obeying them was not a means of joining the people of God but rather a sign that you already were the people of God.

Three aspects of the Law were particularly important by the time of Jesus: circumcision, the Sabbath (the 24 hours of rest from sunset each Friday) and the food laws. All of these had been fiercely defended in recent centuries and under Roman occupation they continued to be vital safeguards of Jewish national identity. They were also helpful 'boundary markers' to delineate who truly belonged to God's people. In a frontier situation like Galilee, where Jews were in frequent contact with non-Jews, any compromise on these issues would be controversial.

Israel also prized two further gifts from God – the 'promised land' and the temple. God had delivered them

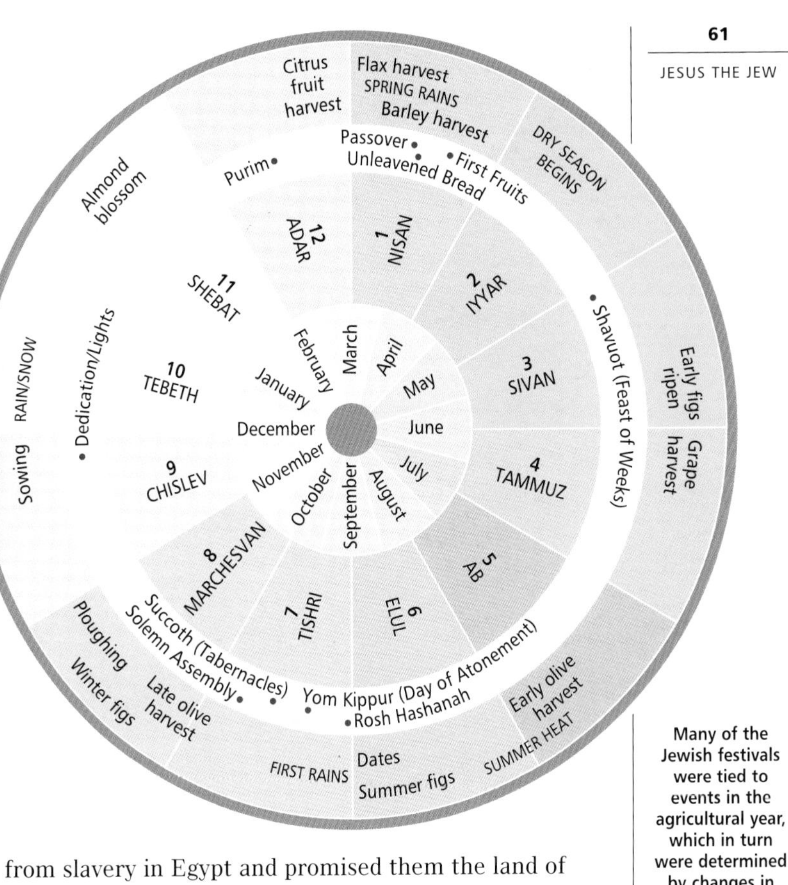

Many of the Jewish festivals were tied to events in the agricultural year, which in turn were determined by changes in the climate.

from slavery in Egypt and promised them the land of Israel – part of God's covenant gift to his people. Because God lived there with them, it was also holy – though the Roman occupation now rendered it 'unclean'. The temple on Mount Zion in Jerusalem was understood to be God's dwelling place and the place for sacrifices. The high point of the year was the Day of Atonement (Yom Kippur). The three major festivals each year were Passover (in March/April), Pentecost or the Festival of Weeks (in May/June) and Tabernacles (in September/October). Technically all Jewish males over the age of 12 were required to attend these festivals each year, but this was difficult for those who lived outside the land in the 'Diaspora' (or 'Dispersion').

As we shall see, there were loyal Jews who were critical of the present temple, but deep down there was a conviction that the Jerusalem temple was indeed a gift from God and he would use it in due course to accomplish his purposes.

Detail of the temple showing the Holy of Holies beyond the Court of Israel. From the 'Holy Land Hotel' model of Jerusalem at the time of the second temple.

What is God going to do?

It should be clear by now that 1st-century Jews could not sustain these beliefs without also hoping that God would

then act decisively to clear up the many ambiguities they raised. The temple was now being rebuilt by pagan King Herod; the land was occupied and ruled by pagan Romans; the evil in the world showed no signs of abating and the chosen people were under continual pressure to compromise. How long could this continue? When was God going to do something about it?

This introduces us to a third big stream within Jewish thought. We have looked at monotheism (there is only one God); we have looked at election (God choosing the people and giving them gracious gifts). Now it is time to introduce 'eschatology' – the Jewish belief that, at the end of the ages, God would bring into this world a new state of affairs – the 'new age' or the 'age to come'.

The Hebrew scriptures were full of the conviction that Israel's God was an active God. History did not go round in circles but was linear: it was going somewhere under God's guiding hand. Hence the frequent predictions or prophecies in the Old Testament. In the book of Isaiah, for example, the people could read various promises that spoke of the restoration of pure worship and Israel's 10 lost tribes, the purification of the temple, and the nations acknowledging the truth of Israel's God. When would these be fulfilled, and how?

Almost certainly there were two further hopes that they longed to see fulfilled. First, there was a growing consensus that God would one day send an 'anointed one' (that is, a Messiah), who would be the agent of deliverance for God's people. 'Anointing' had been one of the marks of Israel's kings, so most people were probably looking for a new king descended from the great King David. Most expected this Messiah to be a military figure who would drive the pagans from the land; others believed he would be a prophetic teacher, or perhaps a priestly figure who would restore true worship.

Secondly, there seems to have been a widespread belief that the exile was not truly over. The people of Israel had gone into exile in Babylon in the

6th century BC, after which a small remnant had returned to Jerusalem. Yet the prophets had seemed to predict something much grander. The exiles were huddled in the vicinity of Jerusalem with much of the land now settled by non-Jews. 'We are slaves today, slaves in the land you gave our fathers' (Nehemiah 9:36). Yes, they were back in the land – in that sense the exile was over – but they were no better than slaves. In that sense, the exile was not over.

There seems, then, to have been a growing belief that God would one day act to 'restore' the fortunes of his people. He would bring his people back from exile. The elaborate and grandiose prophecies about the temple, the return of exiles and the 'ingathering of the nations' would all come to pass.

At the time of Jesus, the nation of Israel was thus on tenterhooks – eager and desperate to see God act to bring this painful drama to its appropriate resolution. Some confirmation of this is found in the New Testament when, for example, we are introduced to people who are described as 'waiting for the consolation of Israel' and looking forward to the 'redemption of Jerusalem' (Luke 2:25, 38). Such language clearly harks back to the prophecies of Isaiah, writing in the face of the exile, where we see very clearly Israel's longing for 'consolation' and 'restoration' (see 'Isaiah's predictions of the end of the exile', page 65).

A 1st-century Jew hearing these texts would be entitled to ask, 'When is all this going to happen?' The texts introduce a whole cluster of hopes associated with a proper 'return from exile': the coming of God as king, the return of the Lord to Zion/Jerusalem and its temple, and the conquest of evil. This was precisely the prophetic programme Jesus then set about to fulfil in his own ministry, when he launched his campaign with the announcement that 'the kingdom of God is near'. Jesus was saying in effect: 'God is at last becoming king. The exile is about to end and Israel will be restored. See now

Isaiah's predictions of the end of the exile

Comfort, comfort my people… Speak tenderly to Jerusalem… Say to the towns of Judah, 'Here is your God!'… How beautiful on the mountains are the feet of those who bring good news… who say to Zion, 'Your God reigns!'… When the Lord returns to Zion, they will see it with their own eyes. Burst into songs of joy together, you ruins of Jerusalem, for the Lord has comforted his people, he has redeemed Jerusalem… All the ends of the earth will see the salvation of our God.

ISAIAH 40:1, 2, 9; 52:7, 8–9, 10

The oldest of the Dead Sea Scrolls found in Qumran. One of the findings among the scrolls was a complete text of Isaiah.

Illumination of a Passover meal from a 14th-century Haggadah.

what God is doing through me – especially as I make my way up to Zion ...!'

This then is the world of Jesus. Above all, this is a story in search of an appropriate ending. The Gospels and the New Testament cannot be understood unless they are seen against this background. They claim that Jesus has brought this story to its fitting climax –

though, as we shall see, he has done so in some surprising ways.

But before we look in detail at the ministry of Jesus, to see how his story fits into this longer story of Israel, we must pause to note the different religious groups that existed in his time. Josephus, the Jewish historian, speaks of four such 'parties' (*Antiquities* 18.1:2–6): the Pharisees, the Sadducees, the Essenes and the Zealots or revolutionaries. Each of these groups came up with different accounts of how this Israel-story was going to unfold. So we will get a much better grasp of the distinctive approach taken by Jesus if we first note the viewpoints of his contemporaries, who were all trying to answer the same question: how and when would God fulfil his promises?

The Pharisees

The Pharisees are the group we encounter most frequently in the story of Jesus, as they had many adherents in Galilee (unlike the Sadducees). They were the largest group, numbering around 6,000.

***Jesus with the Pharisees*. Engraving by Friedrich August Ludy (b. 1823), after a painting by Johann Friedrich Overbeck.**

Although they receive a bad press in the Gospels, they were highly respected in their day. The roots of the Pharisaic movement go back to the time of the Diaspora, when exiled Jews had to develop a spirituality independent of the temple. So Pharisees were closely involved with local synagogues and had a passionate concern to see the precepts of the Torah applied to everyday life. In doing this, they had a high regard for oral traditions which, though not written in the Hebrew scriptures, they believed dated to the time of Moses. Ritual purity and tithing were particularly important. They also had an

'Woe to you, Pharisees! You shut the kingdom of heaven in people's faces... You give a tenth of your spices... But you have neglected the more important matters of the law – justice, mercy and faithfulness... You strain out a gnat but swallow a camel.'

MATTHEW 23:13, 23, 24

increasingly strong belief in the resurrection of the faithful from the dead, which they understood in a fairly physical and material sense.

If they were asked, 'What is God going to do?' they would have highlighted this resurrection hope and stressed the importance of God's people observing his Torah in order to show that they were truly part of God's people. Only those who observed the Torah would be vindicated (or 'justified') by God.

As their name implies ('Pharisees' probably means 'separatists'), their concern was to keep themselves separate from those who were unclean – be they the pagan Romans or the common 'people of the land' who failed to keep properly the commandments of the Torah.

The Dead Sea Scrolls

The Dead Sea Scrolls were discovered in 1947 by some Arab Bedouin, but only recently have their contents been fully published. The scrolls were the precious possession of the Essene community that lived at Qumran by the Dead Sea. As the Roman armies approached in AD 71, the community hid the scrolls in various nearby caves.

There are hundreds of parchment fragments and several complete scrolls, including a complete text of Isaiah (nearly 1,000 years older than our otherwise oldest manuscript, yet almost identical in wording) and numerous commentaries on the Hebrew scriptures. Their writings reveal that this was an exclusively male community, committed to celibacy and strict discipline. They loved the scriptures and longed to see their promises fulfilled in their own day.

Yet it would be a mistake to think of them as 'other-worldly'. Some of them (especially the more conservative 'Shammaite' wing) could also be strongly nationalistic and ready to take up armed resistance against the Roman oppressor. But the Pharisees did not have much sway within Jerusalem's official political structures. The group with political power there was the Sadducees.

The Sadducees

The high priests and most of the Sanhedrin (Judaism's ruling council) were Sadducees. They were the 'establishment' figures of Jesus' day. During the last 100 years, they had gradually developed a way of cooperating with the pagan ruling authorities. As such,

Aerial view of Qumran.

they tended to be very wary of any of their fellow Jews who fostered revolutionary tendencies. They preferred the status quo and did not want their position and security threatened.

It is no coincidence, then, that they had no interest in the doctrine of the resurrection. They preferred life as it was and did not look to their religion for hope of something better. Of all the four groups, this was the one least interested in what God was going to do next. And this, too, tied in with their approach to the scriptures. They only accepted doctrines that could be proved from the Pentateuch (the first five books of the Torah: Genesis to Deuteronomy). Thus all the prophetic writings, which fuelled the popular expectations for God's new future, were neatly excluded from view.

'Then the Sadducees, who say there is no resurrection, came to him with a question... Jesus replied, "Are you not in error because you do not know the scriptures or the power of God?... He is not the God of the dead, but of the living!"'

MARK 12:18, 24, 27

The Essenes

Not surprisingly, there were many who reacted against this attitude (even if it did come from the high priests). The Essenes are the obvious example. This group broke away in the 2nd century BC in reaction to the corruption that it detected in the Jerusalem hierarchy and the temple. They often refer in their writings to the 'Teacher of Righteousness' – probably a priest in the temple who had led the breakaway group.

In deliberate contrast to the temple, they set up various communities around the land with strict patterns for worship and communal life. Members were highly ascetic

and frequently celibate. Almost certainly, the group that lived at Qumran by the Dead Sea were Essenes. It is possible, though disputed, that there was also an Essene group in Jerusalem.

From their writings, found among the Dead Sea Scrolls (see 'The Dead Sea Scrolls', page 68), we can sense their commitment to biblical commentaries and to the task of understanding the prophetic writings. Despite their opposition to the current temple regime, however, they were not revolutionaries but were looking to God to usher in the new age for which they hoped: after a war between the 'sons of light' and the 'sons of darkness' God would establish a reformed temple and pure worship.

The life of Jesus: temptation in the desert

After his baptism in the River Jordan, Jesus went into the nearby Judean desert for an extended period (some '40 days' on his own). In this time of solitude and silence, Jesus prepared for his ministry and prayed through his priorities. We read of his being tempted to doubt his calling and identity, to put God to the test, to seek his own glory through compromise with Satan. It sounds like the story of ancient Israel, who spent 40 years in the wilderness. But this time God has a servant who is faithful: Jesus stands firm, quoting the scriptures, and goes on to Galilee 'in the power of the Spirit' (Luke 4:1–13). Spiritual battles were won here and decisions made that would determine the pattern of his ministry.

'One solitary life': a lone figure in the desert.

Like the Pharisees, they had a firm belief in a future resurrection and were convinced that they alone were the ones whom God would vindicate on that day. In contrast to the Pharisees, however, they tended to withdraw to their monastic settlements and lived in a more apocalyptically charged environment. God had not finished the storyline of Israel, but when the time of fulfilment finally arrived they would be at the forefront of his purposes.

The revolutionaries

For others, all this waiting around for God to act was not to their taste. It was time to take the destiny of Israel into their own hands. The promised land needed to be liberated from the pagans; Jews were to have no king other than God. Eventually this more radical approach came to full expression in the First Jewish Revolt against Rome in AD 66 (when the term 'Zealot' was coined to describe these revolutionaries).

Whenever there was a change of rule, there was a high probability that some revolutionaries would come together to try to change the balance of power. There were violent uprisings at the death of Herod the Great in 4 BC; also in AD 6, when their leader, Judas the Galilean, was hailed as the Messiah. In the years after Jesus, we know the names of several other such 'messianic' figures (such as Simon ben Giora). A hundred years later, the Jews would revolt against Rome once more; and the leader of the rebels – Simon ben Kosiba – would be hailed as the Messiah by the godly Rabbi Akiba.

The frequency of these revolutionary outbursts is a clear sign of the tension that was bubbling away in the land of Jesus' birth. The important point to note, however, is that it was a tension created by biblical hope – by the discrepancy between God's promises in scripture and the reality on the ground. How could the chosen people be in such a powerless state in their own 'promised land'? When would God act to complete what he had promised in the scriptures?

Now we begin to see the significance of Jesus' ministry and his announcement of the 'kingdom of God'. God, he claimed, was about to act at last. We also see why Jesus had to be so careful in the way he presented himself and his message. No doubt the vast majority of Jews were not members of these distinctive 'parties', but most would have shared the desire to be able to observe the Torah peaceably in their own land. They would all be trying to squeeze Jesus' agenda into one of the existing moulds.

But Jesus was going his own way. He was not going the way of detailed attention to ritual purity (like the Pharisees); the way of self-service religion or of compromising with the Romans (like the Sadducees); the way of pietistic withdrawal and escapism (like the Essenes); or the way of military revolution (like the Zealots). Instead, he said, 'Come, follow *me*.'

CHAPTER 6

The Aims of Jesus

Jesus lived in the midst of a people with a sense of divine destiny, a sense of direction, but also a sense of despair. When we forget this and think of Jesus in much more general terms, we are in danger of making his teaching into historically disconnected truths. We must first place his teaching in its right context and take very seriously the evident historical fact that it connected strongly with the live issues of his day – the Jewish issues of the destiny of Israel. He certainly, as we might say, 'struck a chord'.

This sense of destiny, of history moving forwards to an as-yet-to-be-realized goal, is the key thing to note from the beliefs of 1st-century Jews. In this chapter, we will look further at eschatology – the Jewish hope for the dawning

'Jesus came to Galilee, proclaiming the good news of God, and saying, "The time is fulfilled, and the kingdom of God has come near; repent, and believe in the good news."'

MARK 1:14–15

'The kingdom of heaven'

One of the Gospels (Matthew) does not often speak of the 'kingdom of God'; instead Matthew prefers the phrase 'the kingdom of heaven' (see, for example, Matthew 5:3–10). As the most Jewish evangelist, he is simply reflecting Jewish reluctance to use the divine name. 'Heaven' was an oblique way of referring to 'Yahweh', the God of Israel.

But 2,000 years of Gentile church history has tended to 'spiritualize' the phrase. The 'kingdom of heaven' seems to focus us only on the afterlife. Jesus clearly did believe in spiritual realities beyond death, but on his lips 'the kingdom of God' would have had a far more down-to-earth meaning. It was a reality in the here and now: God was becoming king through Jesus, and his kingly rule should now be recognized by all.

of God's new day. Jesus shared this hope, but had his own distinctive ideas about what God was about to do next – and indeed about his own unique place in those divine plans. Jesus' aim was to place himself in the storyline of Israel and then to move the plot forwards into its crucial and long-awaited next phase.

So what were the goals of Jesus' ministry? Within the context of Israel and its destiny for the world, what exactly was he aiming to do? We shall note three overarching aims, each of which is authentically Jewish but also startlingly original. And each of them would get him into trouble.

'The kingdom of God is like a mustard seed, which is the smallest seed you plant in the ground. Yet when planted, it grows and becomes the largest of all garden plants.'

MARK 4:31–32

Aim 1: to announce the kingdom of God

Jesus' first aim is reasonably clear. From the outset of his ministry, Jesus set about proclaiming the 'kingdom of God'. Each of the Synoptic Gospels contains numerous references to this theme.

The 'kingdom of God' meant, quite simply, that God was at last becoming 'king'. This was precisely the good news (or 'gospel') that had been proclaimed in Isaiah. The experience of exile had challenged deeply the faith of Israel. Although the Jews had survived that trauma, the aftermath of exile had left them with a longing for a new day when they would see their God vindicated as the true Lord of the world. Jesus now announced that that day had dawned. The exile, as it were, would now be over properly – once and for all.

As we have seen, this 'kingdom of God' was often politicized by Jesus' contemporaries. Israel looked back to the days of the great kings David and Solomon and longed for God to restore that kingdom. This seemed the obvious way in which Israel's God would reveal his kingship and rule over the world. So if Yahweh was becoming king, that must mean the removal of the pagan Romans: Caesar was not king. It would probably mean also the return of the scattered people of God to the land of Israel and the restoration of pure temple worship.

Statue of Caesar Augustus, the 'lord' of the ancient world.

Jesus' alternative kingdom

But it soon became alarmingly clear that Jesus had other ideas. His kingdom was topsy-turvy and radically different. For a start, he did not propose any military action against Rome, but spoke in positive terms of the Roman forces and peace: 'Give to Caesar what is Caesar's' (Matthew 22:21); 'Blessed are the peacemakers' (Matthew 5:9); if a Roman soldier 'forces you to go one mile, go with him two miles' (Matthew 5:41). This was not the language of liberation. God might be about to be re-enthroned on Mount Zion, but apparently it would not involve an independent Jewish kingdom or the re-installation of Israel's all-too-human kings.

'I have not found anyone in Israel with such great faith... Many will come from the east and west, and will take their places at the feast with Abraham, Isaac and Jacob in the kingdom of heaven. But the subjects of the kingdom will be thrown outside.'

JESUS TO A ROMAN CENTURION, MATTHEW 8:10, 11–12

Jesus' encounter with a Roman centurion early on in his ministry only proved the point. He healed the centurion's servant and then made one of his most shocking statements. In almost treacherous fashion, Jesus announced that there would be a priority in God's kingdom for the pagans, and that the longed-for 'restoration' of Israel to its land might instead be fulfilled when pagans were brought to faith in him – Jesus.

Welcome but warning

Jesus had a distinctive understanding of the kingdom: it was focused on Israel, but it would be for the blessing of the nations. Even the hated Samaritans were not outside its scope (hence his parable of the good Samaritan). It would not look outwardly as impressive as people might hope, but would grow from small beginnings. It would not lead immediately to the eradication of evil (hence his parable about the wheat and weeds continuing to grow alongside one another). It had already begun, but its final consummation might be delayed beyond people's expectation (hence his parable about the 'foolish bridesmaids' caught out by the delay of the bridegroom). Moreover, judging by the nature of Jesus' followers and those he chose to keep company with, it would seemingly include some most unlikely people – a mixed bag of the unimpressive, the religiously 'unclean' and social outcasts.

Worse still, there was more than a hint that this coming of God's kingdom would in fact involve God judging his own people. Israel had experienced this in the exile and longed for the cloud of God's judgment to pass them by. But now this kingdom-prophet from Nazareth clearly implied that Israel was facing another judgment. As in the days of the prophet Amos, they longed for the 'day of the Lord', but it would be a day of darkness. Scholars have counted at least 34 occasions in the Gospels where Jesus threatens the people of his generation with an awesome prospect of judgment. No wonder some compared him to Jeremiah (Matthew 16:14), the prophet who had predicted the first Fall of Jerusalem (to the Babylonians in 587 BC). And, sure enough, 40 years later, at the end of Jesus' generation, Jerusalem would fall once more – this time to the Romans.

'Woe to you who long for the day of the Lord!... That day will be darkness, not light.'

AMOS 5:18

Many of the passages that have since been interpreted as revealing Jesus' belief in God's judgment of all human beings (often rightly) were originally also solemn warnings to Jesus' contemporaries about the impending national disaster. It is as though Jesus is offering a last call to Israel at its final hour, warning of what will happen if they do not repent and respond: 'The axe is already at the root of the trees... Unless you repent, you too will all perish... Daughters of Jerusalem, do not weep for me; weep for yourselves and for your children' (Matthew 3:10; Luke 13:5; 23:28). Both John the Baptist and Jesus were convinced that Israel was now entering the most crucial phase in its history and they warned of a national disaster.

'This is a wicked generation... The men of Nineveh will stand up at the judgment with this generation and condemn it, for they repented at the preaching of Jonah, and now one greater than Jonah is here.'

LUKE 11:29, 32

The last prophet

So the first category for understanding Jesus is that he was an 'eschatological prophet'. This may sound wordy, but it simply means that Jesus saw himself as the one called by God to pronounce the arrival of God's kingdom, which (even if it was manifesting itself in many surprising ways) was indeed the fulfilment of Israel's hopes for the last days. His aim was to speak the ultimate word to Israel.

Jesus seems to have seen himself as the last prophet

of this kind. After him a new state of affairs would be inaugurated. We see this sense of being at the 'shift in the ages' in several places in Jesus' teaching: for example, in his parable of the vineyard when he spoke about all those whom God had sent to Israel in the past – but 'last of all' he sent his 'beloved son' (Mark 12:6).

This last passage also hints that Jesus, while a prophet, saw himself as much more than that. This will lead us on to ask in a moment the harder questions about who exactly Jesus was claiming to be. Yet at this stage, our point is this: Jesus was interpreted by his contemporaries in 'prophetic' categories (see, for example, Luke 7:16). He was seen as a prophet announcing God's kingdom. And, given that it was over 400 years since Israel had experienced such prophetic ministry, this in itself was quite enough to cause people to sit up and take notice.

'From the days of John the Baptist until now, the kingdom of heaven has been forcefully advancing... For all the Prophets and the Law prophesied until John.'

MATTHEW 11:12, 13

Aim 2: to reveal his mysterious identity

But Jesus had not just come to announce the arrival of God's kingdom; he was himself inaugurating it. His arrival was its arrival. Jesus came with the kingdom and the kingdom came with Jesus. The two are inseparable.

So the question about the presence of the kingdom turns out to be a question about the person of Jesus. Surrounded by Pharisees on one occasion he dared to state that 'the kingdom of God is within you' (Luke 17:21). The kingdom had arrived because Jesus himself had arrived. He seems to have seen himself not just as the herald of the kingdom, but as the king himself.

'But if I drive out demons by the Spirit of God, then the kingdom of God has come upon you.'

MATTHEW 12:28

This is where Jesus' miraculous works of power fit in: his powerful healings, his feeding of the crowds, his evident mastery of nature and even death. They were dramatic signs that God's kingly rule was breaking into human affairs in a powerful new way – in and through Jesus.

So the kingdom turns out to be all about *Jesus*. This underlies one of the great paradoxes of the Gospels. We keep hearing Jesus talking about the 'kingdom of God', and it sounds self-effacing. Jesus is pointing attention away from himself and on to God instead – or so it seems at first glance. But the more we read, the more we realize he is using this as a cryptic way of pointing to himself. He is daringly egocentric.

Jesus' calling of the first disciples was marked by a momentous catch of fish. Attributed to Duccio di Buoninsegna (c. 1255–c. 1318).

On one occasion, for example, he is asked a question about the number of people who will be 'saved' and enjoy the 'feast in the kingdom of God'. He answers by telling a story about 'the owner of the house' closing the door, with people then pleading to be let in (Luke 13:22–30). It is fairly clear that the 'owner' represents God, the king in the 'kingdom'. But then the people in the story, who have been thrust outside, say, 'But we ate and drank with you, and you taught in our streets.' Suddenly it becomes clear that Jesus is talking about his contemporaries (indeed some of his hearers right at that moment), warning them that merely having Jesus teaching in their streets will not be enough to save them when they meet again at the door of God's kingdom: 'Away from me you evil-doers!' Chilling stuff, but also mind-boggling. Jesus is identifying himself with the owner of God's house: he is the king in this kingdom of God.

This kind of thing happens frequently. Jesus claims to hold the keys to the 'mysteries of the kingdom' (Mark 4:11). He turns out to be the 'bridegroom' at the messianic banquet (Mark 2:19). His practice of eating meals with sinners was intended to symbolize God's welcome to the people of Jesus at the messianic banquet (Luke 14–15). On another occasion, he told a parable about himself as the 'Son of man' in his glory, dividing the sheep from the goats. But the parable goes on instead to talk about 'the king' (Matthew 25:31–46). Jesus himself is the king. And indeed 'Son of man' was a far from neutral title: in Daniel's heavenly vision the Son of man represented the 'saints of the Most High' (Daniel 7:9). This was an exalted status, not a menial one. The Son of man represents Israel to God.

'Whoever welcomes me welcomes the One who sent me.'

MATTHEW 10:40

But what this then means is that you cannot praise Jesus for his exalted ethical and religious teaching about God's kingdom-values while ignoring his claims about himself. They are inextricably connected; they stand or fall together. Some hope you can, as it were, go through the garden of Jesus' teaching, plucking here and there an ethical flower, but these plucked flowers will wither when removed from their original context. To be sure, Jesus' teaching included ethical teaching of the highest order, but the primary focus of Jesus' teaching was not ethics, but eschatology – that is, he wanted people to recognize what God was doing in fulfilment of his promises, and *who it was* that he was doing this through. Jesus was aiming not only to announce the kingdom, but actually to bring it about – in and through himself. Inevitably, then, he had to draw some attention to his own mysterious identity.

Jesus the secret Messiah

The category that was uppermost in the minds of most of Jesus' contemporaries at the time was that of the 'Messiah'. From Judas the Galilean (AD 6) onwards there was a string of messianic claimants in 1st-century Palestine. The Messiah was widely expected to be an anointed 'king' of some kind. So if someone like Jesus suddenly came along announcing the arrival of God's kingdom and performing actions of dramatic power, it would not take long before someone would raise the inevitable question: was this kingdom-announcer himself the awaited Messiah–king?

The fact that Jesus saw himself as the apparent 'king of the kingdom' immediately suggests that he would indeed have seen himself as the Messiah. In Jewish thought, the 'Messiah' was presumed to be a human figure, not a divine one. It was not then, as some have suggested, automatically 'weird' to think you were the Messiah.

Jesus had to be careful, however, as he advanced his messianic claim. If he was the true Messiah–king, it was evident that his kingdom was radically different from popular expectations. This meant he had to keep people guessing. If people publicly hailed him as Messiah, they would either try to squeeze him into their job description for the Messiah, or, if he resisted, could become disillusioned and hostile.

'Jesus, knowing that they intended to... make him king by force, withdrew again into the hills by himself.'

JOHN 6:15

Jesus' strategy was what is now known as the

'messianic secret' – he only hinted at his Messiahship, and he asked those who knew to keep the secret. Given the political scenario we have sketched, there is no need to see this sceptically. It was a necessary survival strategy. Only in this way could Jesus gradually advance his claim to be the true, but different Messiah. He had to 'reinvent the term', accepting the title but giving its meaning a whole new content.

'Whenever the evil spirits saw him, they recognized him. But he gave them strict orders not to tell who he was.'
MARK 3:11–12

Another one of Jesus' aims, then, was to build the case, bit by bit, for his own alternative Messiahship, so that in due course, when people could affirm his claim in this new Jesus-defined sense, there would be ample evidence that Jesus himself had intended it this way. So it is appropriate that the mid-point climax of Mark's Gospel is Peter's hesitant but clear confession: 'You are the

Jesus only hinted at his mysterious identity – God's Messiah, the 'Son of man', who would come in glory and judge the world. *Christ Glorified in the Court of Heaven* by Fra Angelico (c. 1387–1455).

Messiah!' (Mark 8:29). Sufficient hints have been given. Now, with only the disciples in attendance, Jesus owns the truth and shares his secret.

His second aim was coming to fulfilment: the mystery of his identity was being revealed. He was the Messiah – and even more than the Messiah. He was not just implementing the promises of God. In some strange sense, he was also the presence of God.

Aim 3: to perform the messianic task

As Peter soon found out to his embarrassment, successfully identifying Jesus as Messiah did not mean you now fully understood what he was going to do next. The disciples must have been so excited: they were in the chosen company of the Messiah; it was time for the revolution to

start and for the march on Jerusalem! But Jesus started talking about the need to 'suffer many things' and die. He told them that his followers must be ready to 'take up their cross' (Mark 8:31–34). The divine plan seemed to have gone strangely wrong. What was happening?

The suffering servant

Jesus had found in the scriptures a deeper, more mysterious, theme. In the book of Isaiah, intertwined with passages about the restoration of Israel, there were four songs about a mysterious 'servant'. The last of these spoke of a suffering servant who by his death would bring about forgiveness for 'many' (Isaiah 53:11). In some ways, this 'servant' seemed to be identified with the people of Israel; in other ways the passage seemed to point to a solitary individual. Jesus now interpreted this passage in a bold new way – unlike anyone before him.

He brought together this servant motif (the innocent sufferer) with the Messiah (the royal conqueror) and moulded them into a strange unity. The Messiah would win Israel's battle, but it would be through apparent defeat. This Messiah–servant would be an individual, but would also represent God's people, Israel. And he claimed that role for himself.

Jesus continues to make clear statements about the necessity of his death in accordance with prophecy, deliberately using Isaiah's terminology when he speaks of 'giving his life as a ransom for many' (Mark 10:45). From his own reading of scripture Jesus was convinced that the 'Messiah had to suffer' (Luke 24:26) and he resolved to put this into effect. This messianic claimant could not get puffed up with his own importance. On the contrary, he had an awesome task to fulfil, which meant going to the 'lowest of the low'.

'See, my servant will act wisely… He was despised and rejected… Surely he took up our infirmities and carried our sorrows… But he was pierced for our transgressions… We all, like sheep, have gone astray; and the Lord has laid on him the iniquity of us all… By knowledge of him my righteous servant will justify many, and he will bear their iniquities.'

ISAIAH 52:13; 53:3, 4, 5, 6, 11

The real enemy

What is going on here? The Messiah was, above all, expected to implement God's rule by overcoming God's enemies. At the time, people presumed that this 'enemy' must be Rome. But Jesus clearly thought differently. For Jesus, the real enemy was evil itself, personified in the Bible as 'Satan'. This was the ultimate enemy who had to be defeated.

People had hoped that Israel, the 'light to the nations', might be able to solve the problem of the world's sinfulness and rebellion against God. But Jesus knew Israel had failed. God's calling had evolved into a cause for pride and exclusivism. As a result, there was a need for a new Israel and a true Israelite, one untainted by sin, to take on the issue single-handedly – like a new David fighting Goliath.

People also thought the problem to be solved was Israel's exile, but the real problem was the cause of that exile – human sinfulness. This was the real enemy. So Jesus now took up where Israel had left off. If sin and rebellion must necessarily lead to God's judgment, then Jesus would bear the penalty. He bore the 'curse' of God's wrath, so that sin could be dealt with – forgiven – and put away. Only in this way could the exile caused by sin be brought to an end and the good news of God's forgiveness be published to the world. Israel will then have become the means of blessing for the nations.

'The Christ will suffer and rise from the dead on the third day, and repentance and forgiveness of sins will be preached in his name to all nations, beginning at Jerusalem.'

LUKE 24:46–47

A death for the whole world

How did Jesus view the world and his role within it? All along, Israel was called to be 'a light to the nations', but Israel was caught up in the sin of the world. So there comes to the heart of Israel one who himself is the true Israel, representing the heart of the nation, doing for the world what Israel could no longer do.

On the cross, he will bear the sins of Israel, bringing Israel out of its sin-caused exile, but he will also bear the sins of the wider world. Jesus will bear the brunt of human sin and Israel's sin, but he will also take away the judgment they deserve in God's sight. In so doing, he will conquer sin and death, and make available to all the forgiveness of sins.

This explains what we see going on in Jesus' ministry. He was announcing the coming of divine judgment upon evil and Israel's sin in particular, but he also believed it was his messianic role to bear that judgment in his own body on the cross. Only so could Israel's sin be removed; only so could the sin of the world be dealt with; only so could Satan be defeated.

If Israel was still in exile because of her sin, then this Messiah who represented Israel must enter into that exile and judgment too, bear that sin and then come out the other side – the true victor in the messianic battle. The longed-for restoration of Israel would then come about through the resurrection of Israel's Messiah. And it would be implemented through

***The life of Jesus*: the synagogue at Nazareth**

The earliest written evidence for synagogue activity within Judaism comes from the Gospels. The local synagogue would have played an important role in Jesus' upbringing. It was a place for worship, debate and study – a place at the heart of ordinary community life.

Reconstructed synagogue in 'Nazareth Village'.

At the synagogue in Nazareth, Jesus gave his famous 'Nazareth manifesto' (Luke 4:16–30). Luke deliberately places this incident at the start of Jesus' public ministry. Jesus read a prophecy from Isaiah ('the Spirit of the Lord is upon me to announce good news to the poor...': Isaiah 61), and then announced that it was being fulfilled in their own hearing. It sounded good – though a bit presumptuous for a man who had grown up in their village streets. But then he shocked them by announcing that, through his own ministry, God would bless those outside Israel. This was too much. So they tried to manhandle him out of the village to throw him over one of the nearby cliffs. The kingdom was coming, but not in the way they wanted.

the proclamation of this Messiah's kingship over all the earth.

And what of the Gentile world? Jesus' death would be not just for the sins of Israel but for the sins of the whole world. The good news of divine forgiveness could go out to all the world because God himself had truly dealt with human sin – in all its manifestations, everywhere.

Jesus and the cross

The above explanation may at first seem alien to our ears. But, with its Jewish focus on the role of Israel, it is arguably more likely to have been the view of Jesus himself. It has often been argued that Jesus simply could not have contemplated his own death and its connection to human sin; this is all deemed to be a later invention of the church. The advantage of our presentation here is that we can begin to build a case that would make perfect sense for a 1st-century Palestinian Jew.

'He is the atoning sacrifice for our sins, and not only for ours but also for the sins of the whole world.'

1 JOHN 2:2

At the same time, of course, it then paves the way, without any contradiction, for the apostles' explanation of the cross. Jesus and the apostles are giving us between them 'two sides of the same coin' – one side being Jesus' viewpoint before his death, working within the thought-frame of Israel; the other side being that of the apostles, who were beginning to set Jesus' work in a more universal context with the gift of hindsight.

It may also increase our respect for Jesus himself. This was an agonizing vocation to discover and then to enact. No one around Jesus would understand what he was really doing until it was too late. And the only way Jesus could verify his calling was to abandon himself totally and utterly into the hands of God – the God whom he dared to call his 'Father'. It would take awesome trust. What if he was wrong?

CHAPTER 7

The Challenges of Jesus

Jesus clearly had an agenda, a task he had to fulfil. So as we consider some of his other teachings we must keep his mission in mind. His words are a commentary on his work. They express not just his character, not just his vision of God, but his own mission and the dynamic activity of his God.

Jesus' teaching is nothing if not challenging. We can only touch on it briefly under three headings: the challenge to acknowledge his unique role, join his new people and live his new life.

'If anyone is ashamed of me and my words in this adulterous and sinful generation, the Son of man will be ashamed of him when he comes in his Father's glory and with the holy angels.'

MARK 8:38

Challenge 1: to acknowledge Jesus

The Gospels contain urgent calls for people to recognize Jesus for who he is. 'Repent' is his opening command and it is repeated again and again: 'I have not come to call the righteous, but sinners to repentance' (Luke 5:32). If God's people want to be restored, then they must recognize the spiritual crisis within Israel and their own part in it. They must abandon their own agendas, turn from their sin, and then in daring trust they must 'follow' Jesus (Mark 1:17). In other words, they needed to believe in Jesus as the one through whom Israel's God was now uniquely at work. And people did follow him, setting out on the road of risky discipleship with Jesus: 'If anyone would come after me, he must deny himself and take up his cross and follow me... Whoever loses his life for me and for the gospel will save it' (Mark 8:34, 35).

The issue becomes even sharper as Jesus mounts his final challenge in Jerusalem and is expressly questioned

Several of Jesus' followers were fishermen on Lake Galilee.

about his authority (Luke 20–21). He describes himself as the vineyard owner's 'son' who should not be killed, also as King David's 'Lord' who will sit at God's right hand. He is the 'Son of man' who will be vindicated 'with power and great glory' before whom we will stand, and who will be found 'seated at the right hand of the mighty God'. As his ministry came to a close, Jesus did not hold back from confessing his own identity and he warned people that they needed to acknowledge this. He was looking for those who would identify with him and who would recognize both his identity and his mission.

'He called his disciples to him and chose twelve of them.'
LUKE 6:13

This can be seen in his Last Supper with his disciples, when he takes bread and wine and invites his followers to identify with him in his forthcoming death. If some have questioned whether Jesus could have consciously planned his death, the Last Supper puts these doubts to one side. It was a powerful symbol, an enacted parable, of his imminent death. It was an invitation to see Jesus as the one who fulfilled Jewish hopes by being the Passover lamb – a sacrifice offered to turn aside God's wrath. It was, above all, a challenge to encounter Jesus personally and to identify with him in his death. Jesus had taught many things, and done some amazing acts, but what he wanted his followers to remember him for, more than anything else, was his death.

Jesus was challenging people to see his unique role in God's purposes and to acknowledge the achievement of his death for them as individuals. This would require people putting their trust (or 'faith') in Jesus and also 'repenting' – that is, abandoning their own agendas and acknowledging their sin, for which his death would prove to be God's remedy.

Challenge 2: to join his new people

Jesus was looking for committed followers. He was not simply teaching a few new principles about the religious life and hoping that some within Israel would begin to incorporate these into their own religious beliefs and systems. Jesus was initiating or founding a new messianic renewal movement with himself as its head. As is indicated through all his teaching on discipleship and on the cost of following him, Jesus was calling into being a new people who would be known as his followers.

But how would these followers of Jesus relate to the wider people of God, the nation of Israel? The devastating answer was that Jesus was reconstituting Israel around himself. In his own person (as the Messiah, the king, the Son of man), there were important senses in which he himself was the representative of the nation and was himself Israel. But now, by extension, his followers were to be 'Israel'. Thus he was gathering together a new community, which would be the true embodiment of Israel.

What reveals this most clearly is his choice of 12 disciples (or apostles) to be his 'inner cabinet'. Though there remain some uncertainties about their names, the tradition is fixed. Jesus chose not 11 or 13, but 12 disciples. The signal was clear. The people of Israel had originally consisted of 12 tribes; people longed for the 10 lost tribes to be regathered and for Israel to be restored to its full complement. Jesus now, in both symbol and practice, began the reconstitution of Israel. Picking up the idea of the faithful 'remnant', he tells his disciples that they are God's 'little flock' to whom God has given the kingdom (Luke 12:32).

'When the Son of man sits on his glorious throne, you who have followed me will also sit on twelve thrones, judging the twelve tribes of Israel.'

MATTHEW 19:28

Jesus, then, was not just challenging individuals in their response to him. He was also calling forth a new community and asking people to join this community. While being thoroughly loyal to his overarching Jewish commitments, he was casting a vision for a new people of God – a new people, with himself at its very centre.

This again explains the hostility that Jesus encountered among his own people. It was not just his hints at his own identity that stuck in people's throats. It was also his agenda for Israel, and the radical belief that somehow he had the authority to refashion Israel around himself and around a startlingly new set of criteria.

In many ways, because of this, it would prove easier in due course for non-Jews to believe in him than his own people. They had less to lose. After all, those outside the 'people of God' would rejoice to be included; but those who thought they already were the people of God would baulk at having to reapply for membership. But this had already been hinted at in John the Baptist's call for Israel to undergo his baptism. There was a call to start again, an announcement that Israel was being restored by being

Jesus kept 'open table' with all alike. *Christ at Supper with Simon the Pharisee*, probably by Luca di Tomme (15th century).

reconstituted. People did not like this, as is evident from the numerous conflict stories in the Gospels. In due season Jesus would be accused of subverting the nation and of being a false prophet who was 'leading Israel astray' (Luke 23:2).

The 'new people' of Jesus did indeed look quite different. In particular, Jesus was placing himself at the very centre – the place that should surely have been reserved for Yahweh himself or perhaps for those central symbols of his divine presence (namely, his Torah or his temple).

Who was welcome?

Then there was the issue of who could join his new people. Jesus was not as fussy as some thought be should be. This holy man kept company with the oddest people. His main group of disciples, from a Pharisaic point of view at least, were probably already 'beyond the pale', as they did not observe the Torah sufficiently. But then Jesus accepted within his chosen band a tax collector, a man called Levi. Jesus' reputation would have plummeted – and all the more so when he then accepted Levi's invitation to a party that thronged with other tax collectors and notorious 'sinners'. Jesus agreed with the Pharisees' description of these people as 'sinners', but assured them that such 'sinners' were precisely the ones whom he had come for. The kingdom had come, but for all the wrong people. It did not go down all that well.

'John the Baptist came neither eating bread nor drinking wine, and you say, "He has a demon." The Son of man came eating and drinking and you say, "Here is a glutton and a drunkard, a friend of tax collectors and 'sinners'."'

LUKE 7:33–34

Worse was to follow. Jesus dared to touch the 'untouchable' lepers and let himself be touched by a prostitute. He made positive noises about the Jews' arch-enemies, the Samaritans, and did not speak out against the Romans. In his ministry, he might be concentrating for strategic reasons on the 'lost sheep of the house of Israel' but he clearly did not exclude non-Jews entirely from his sight (hence his conversation with a woman from Syro-Phoenicia). And Jesus continued to keep table with some questionable characters and to gain a reputation sharply at odds with that of his more austere contemporary, John the Baptist.

The entrance requirements for Jesus' new kingdom-people seemed remarkably lax. 'This man welcomes sinners, and eats with them,' the Pharisees noted. What is more, he claimed that in so doing he was only reflecting the character and purposes of Israel's God. The master of the messianic banquet wanted all the seats to be taken, by the good and bad alike, by the 'poor, the crippled, the lame and the blind'. He was the God who welcomed back the 'prodigal son' and rejoiced over just 'one sinner who repented'.

Badges of belonging

What about the new boundary markers of this group? How would this new people of Jesus be defined and recognized?

Judaism defined itself by some very obvious boundary markers, which fenced off quite clearly the members of the house of Israel. These symbols or 'badges' of national identity kept the Jewish people socially distinct and grew out of their commitment to the Torah. They included, most obviously, Sabbath observance, Jewish food laws and circumcision. Other key components were less visible, but equally as important – such as their commitment to the family and nation and to the Jerusalem temple.

Yet these were precisely the things that Jesus seemed to bring into question. In a frontier-place like Galilee, where preserving Jewish distinctiveness was vital, Jesus' attitudes would have stirred up a hornet's nest. These were things on which good Jews must not start to compromise. To break ranks would cause the national identity to unravel.

It was not, of course, that Jesus disagreed with the Torah. As we can see from various episodes, his own attitude to the authority and truth of the scriptures was beyond question. It was simply that God was now doing a new thing – as indeed the Law and the Prophets had themselves predicted. This was the era of fulfilment.

That's why Jesus spoke of his goal of fulfilling the Law and made a cryptic reference to something being 'accomplished'. When that came to pass, when everything to which the Law looked forward had arrived, then the story of Israel would have moved into a whole new phase. And in that new phase, new rules would apply and some of the old boundary markers would become redundant – not because they had been bad, but simply because their time had come.

This last point is crucial. Jesus' debates with those who criticized him must not be wrenched out of the context of eschatology. Jesus' point so often is not to do with the things themselves, but to try and point people to the 'signs of the times'. This is a new season. With the coming of Jesus, Israel is now moving into the messianic age. Jesus' contentions over the Sabbath and food laws, for example, are all tied up with his view of his own place in Israel's timetable. They are provocative announcements that things are about to change.

'Do not think that I have come to abolish the Law or the Prophets; I have not come to abolish them but to fulfil them… Not the smallest letter, not the least stroke of a pen, will by any means disappear from the Law until everything is accomplished.'

MATTHEW 5:17, 18

Hallmarks of a new age

So, first, Jesus challenges the Sabbath. There were strict limitations on what work could be done on the Sabbath, but Jesus encourages his disciples to pluck corn and cites King David as his precedent. There is more than a hint that Jesus sees himself in the same situation as the young David – destined to be king, but not yet recognized. He caps it all by claiming to be the 'Lord of the Sabbath' (Mark 2:23–28). On another occasion, he argues that, far from being irregular, it is perfectly proper that his healings should take place on the Sabbath, the day which celebrated release from captivity and work. The hint is that Jesus was himself bringing about God's intended Sabbath rest for his people.

Then he challenged the food laws. The purity codes were all about keeping people separate, but Jesus worked with a more inclusive vision. Hence his radical statement (delivered indoors privately where only his disciples could hear): 'Don't you see that nothing that enters a person from the outside can make them "unclean"?' (Mark 7:18). In one sentence, Jesus was undermining the whole structure on which the food laws were based. As Mark comments, he was declaring 'all foods "clean"'. He was opening up a way that would enable Jews and non-Jews to sit together at common table, for both the 'clean' and the 'unclean' to meet. Although Jesus seems not to have spoken explicitly about the issue of circumcision, the general drift of his thinking is becoming quite clear.

He also questioned the ultimate loyalty due to one's blood family. In a Jewish context, Jesus' words on this theme are shocking: 'Whoever does God's will is my brother and sister and mother' (Mark 3:35). Jesus is not saying family is unimportant, but there is now a greater loyalty – the family or 'kinship group' of Jesus himself. And Israel will have to recognize that being a member of the 'people of God' is no longer going to be defined in terms of family and race, but rather through loyalty to Jesus.

'I have come to set a man against his father, and a daughter against her mother… Whoever loves father or mother more than me is not worthy of me.'

MATTHEW 10:35, 37

Finally, Jesus had a radical approach to the temple. Again this was not because it had somehow been a mistake, but primarily because its time had come. It was a place tainted with various corruptions, but Jesus' prophetic act, when he overturned the table of the money changers, was motivated even more by the desire to signal his own authority and what he had come to bring – the age of messianic fulfilment. In that new age, there would no longer be a need for such a temple, and Jesus himself would offer a far more effective sacrifice. In fulfilment of the Old Testament teaching (that God's forgiveness was brought about through a sacrificial death), Jesus would offer his own body on a cross. From now on Jesus, not the temple, would be the means of receiving forgiveness from God.

'I tell you that one greater than the temple is here.'

MATTHEW 12:6

In all these ways, Jesus challenged some of the fundamental identity markers of Israel. He was thoroughly Jewish, but subversively so – because he was announcing the dawn of a new age. Israel was meant to be the 'light of the world' but these boundary markers had effectively caused her to keep her light hidden. Now that role was being transferred through him to his disciples and it was time for the light to be let out at last: 'You are the light of the world' (Matthew 5:14). All those things that kept Israel separate from the surrounding nations would no longer be required. The light no longer needed to be conserved – it could be spread.

It was a daring strategy, to say the least. It could easily be misconstrued as disloyalty or dangerous radicalism. For Jesus, however, it was all about revealing the dawning of the new age in which the 'people of God' would be redefined. Jesus was reconstituting Israel around his own person. He wanted his followers to be part of a new people, for whom the one boundary marker was now faith in him, Israel's Messiah.

'You are the salt of the earth.'

MATTHEW 5:13

Challenge 3: to live his new life

Finally, we note Jesus' challenge to live life in a new way. How was life to be lived in this new Jesus-centred kingdom? Jesus' ethics have obviously been discussed in minute detail and we can only say a few brief words about them. They are vitally important and must be considered in their kingdom context.

This means, for example, that we cannot treat the Sermon on the Mount (perhaps the most famous body of Jesus' teaching) as a set of timeless ethics. Instead, it is Jesus' challenge to his would-be disciples, when set amidst many possible alternatives, of how they should be the true people of God. This is Jesus' kingdom manifesto, as it were, at the launch of his campaign. It outlines the 'narrow way', compared with the much broader path taken by the majority and warns that other agendas on the market are so much 'building on sand'. It is an urgent warning of how to live in the light of the coming judgment. It is a statement of Jesus' alternative values, his deeper understanding of the Old Testament and his challenge to the Israel of his day to adopt Jesus' way for being God's people before it is too late.

'Love your enemies... that you may be children of your Father in heaven.'

MATTHEW 5:44, 45

If this sermon is counter-cultural in the 21st century, it is only so because it was also counter-cultural within the Israel of Jesus' own day. Because Jesus' kingdom was so different from the kingdom expectations of his contemporaries, so too are his ethics. The kingdom belongs not to those who are self-confident but to the 'poor in spirit', not to the zealots but to the peacemakers, not to the Pharisees but to those who 'hunger and thirst for righteousness' and know the meaning of mercy.

'Everyone who hears these words of mine and does not put them into practice is like a fool who built his house on sand.'

MATTHEW 7:26

Jesus' kingdom is one that takes the word of God in the scriptures very seriously, rather than letting human traditions blunt its challenge. So it requires the secret inner motivations of the heart to be examined and is not satisfied with external rectitude. Jesus is not looking for those who only call him 'Lord' (itself, by the way, a staggering expectation from the human Jesus), but for those who 'do the will of my Father in heaven'. If we hear Jesus' words, we are to obey them and put them into practice.

Jesus' kingdom also finds that at the heart of the Law

The Sermon on the Mount

Blessed are the poor in spirit, for theirs is the kingdom of heaven.
Blessed are those who mourn, for they will be comforted.
Blessed are the meek, for they will inherit the earth.
Blessed are those who hunger and thirst for righteousness, for they will be filled.

So begins the most famous sermon of all time – Jesus' 'Sermon on the Mount' (Matthew 5–7). Matthew has drawn together Jesus' teaching into a short manifesto for those who would be disciples in his new kingdom; Jesus is like a new Moses bringing the Law from a new Mount Sinai. It is in keeping with the Old Testament, but it challenges more deeply, and overturns many of the expectations of Jesus' hearers – now as then.

The Church of the Beatitudes, with Lake Galilee in the background.

is the law of love. This is God's essential nature. Those who are in the kingdom of Jesus are to be those who love. The new 'people of God' is not to be marked by a self-righteous dismissal of those outside, justifying its hatred to its enemies because they are supposedly God's enemies: 'God causes his sun to rise on the evil and the good.'

'Fear him who... has power to throw you into hell.'
LUKE 12:5

The holiness of God

At the heart of Jesus' ethical vision, then, stands this seemingly paradoxical vision of God's holiness combined with God's love. It is worth drawing out these two different strands in other parts of his teaching.

The God known and proclaimed by Jesus is the same God as Yahweh, the God of Israel. If Jesus adds to that Hebraic understanding of God, it is an expansion, not a correction. We see in Jesus' life and teaching a deeper penetration into the character of this 'Holy One of Israel'. The God of Jesus was morally perfect, radically opposed to evil, and upright in all his actions.

'Be perfect, therefore, as your heavenly Father is perfect.'
MATTHEW 5:48

In the Lord's Prayer, Jesus prays that God's holy name be 'hallowed' or revered throughout the earth. His careful choice of language, often using 'heaven' to avoid the use of the divine name, underscores his Jewish reverence for

The Lord's Prayer

Jesus' relationship with his Father gave his disciples a new vision of prayer (Luke 11:1–4; cf. Matthew 6:9–13). The disciples asked, 'Lord, teach us to pray.' Jesus replied, 'This is how you should pray:

"Our Father in heaven, hallowed be your name,
your kingdom come, your will be done
on earth as it is in heaven.
Give us today our daily bread. Forgive us our debts,
as we also have forgiven our debtors.
And lead us not into temptation,
but deliver us from the evil one."'

God's utter holiness. Like the Hebrew prophets of old, Jesus urges a radical obedience to the covenant and warns solemnly of the consequences for those who do not. Jerusalem herself will not be spared. And individuals, too, need to reckon with the justice of God. Jesus warns Israel, and warns us, of the reality of God's holiness. Holiness is required of the people of God.

The love of God

But God's holiness is inseparable from God's love. The way Jesus shared his table with all and sundry was an enacted parable of God's welcome to the sinful. Holiness was important but you could still eat with Jesus. For God's nature was identical with that of the 'prodigal father' who welcomes back his profligate son with open arms. Jesus

'His father saw him and was filled with compassion for him; he... threw his arms around him and kissed him.'

LUKE 15:20

Return of the Prodigal Son **by Rembrandt van Rijn (1606–69).**

introduces us by these teachings to a God who comes out to meet us in love, inviting us home.

And 'Father' was indeed the right word to use of this God. In all his prayers, apart from one (the cry of despair on the cross), Jesus addresses God as 'Father'. 'Abba' was the colloquial word used by both children and grown-ups of their father, an intimate word that acknowledged both his love and his authority. Jesus now spoke to God in this vein, and encouraged his followers to do the same. It was not entirely without parallel within Jewish thought, but it was exceedingly rare. It became the heartbeat of prayer for Jesus' followers – not least as they responded to the new demonstration of God's love in the life and death of Jesus.

'I have come to seek and to save what was lost.'

LUKE 19:10

In due course, the coming of Jesus would itself be seen

***The life of Jesus*: the mountains in the north**

At a critical point in his ministry, Jesus left Lake Galilee and went to the far north of the country. In the region around Caesarea Philippi, Jesus asked his disciples privately that most important question: 'Who do you say that I am?' 'You are the Messiah!' responded Peter. Jesus commended him but then spoke of the 'Son of man' going up to Jerusalem to die. Now that the disciples were sensing his identity, they must also understand his quite distinctive mission.

Shrine niches in Caesarea Philippi.

A week later he took Peter, James and John up a mountainside (almost certainly the lower slopes of the nearby Mount Hermon). There Jesus was 'transfigured'. He was seen in glory talking with Moses and Elijah, two of the greatest Old Testament prophets. Peter tried to speak, but the divine voice broke in: 'This is my Son, whom I love. Listen to him!'

as the clearest demonstration of God's love. Jesus had described the compassion of the 'good Samaritan' who, despite being an enemy to the Jews, showed mercy and acted as a true neighbour to the Jewish person in distress. Looking back on it afterwards, Jesus' followers could see that Jesus himself had been the 'good Samaritan' towards them, acting as 'neighbour' to them in their need. His whole life demonstrated the holiness and the love of God. And his cross then brought these two into perfect harmony – as Jesus affirmed God's judgment but also the full demonstration of his love.

Those who accepted Jesus' call were thus challenged to live in the light of these awesome realities, coming to know and then to imitate the God of perfect holiness and love. It was a staggering calling, then as now. Jesus'

Jesus' transfiguration probably took place on the lower slopes of Mount Hermon, the peak of which is covered in snow for most of the year.

followers are to be signs of the reign of God in a broken world. But with the calling comes divine aid. For Jesus' God is also the generous and gracious God who gives 'good gifts to his children'.

The witness of John

We have, of course, only touched the surface. But there is one final thing to note. In the last two chapters, little has been used from the Gospel of John. This was not to dismiss its slightly different and more 'spiritual' account as evidence for the Jesus of history, but rather to show how, even in the Synoptic Gospels, we come face to face with a Jesus who makes staggering claims for himself.

John's Jesus, too, must be placed against the backdrop of Israel. He, too, comes to fulfil that story in his life, death and resurrection. There is a greater emphasis on the issue of Jesus' person and especially on his identity as God's 'Son', but that theme can be found in the Synoptic Gospels as well. It is there in the story of Jesus' baptism, and there in the event they all place at the climax of Jesus' ministry in Galilee – the 'transfiguration'. So the Fourth Gospel may simply be the result of John allowing the transfiguration, which he himself witnessed somewhere on the slopes of Mount Hermon, to shape the whole of his narrative: 'We have seen his glory, the glory as of a father's only son' (John 1:14). And John would agree with the Synoptic writers about the essence of Jesus' teaching: acknowledge the uniqueness of Jesus, follow him, and you will walk in the ways of 'eternal life'.

CHAPTER 8

The Road to Jerusalem

Jesus was proving to be a controversial figure. Galilee was always a hotbed of unrest, but now this preacher from Nazareth was adding fuel to the flames. In the light of his authoritative but subversive teaching, his sense of his own identity and destiny, his acts of power and his challenge to accepted conventions, there was now an inevitable question: where would it all end?

In Jesus' world, there was only one answer to that question. It could only end in Jerusalem.

From Galilee to Jerusalem

Jerusalem, as we have already seen, was the central hub of Jewish life, the focus of Israel's hopes. The Jews in Galilee, though themselves often despised by the residents of Jerusalem, were by and large fiercely loyal towards the city. This was their 'holy city', their mother city. Large numbers of them, for example, would go to Jerusalem for Passover each spring. So, if you were doing the kind of things that Jesus was, you would at some point have to make a bid for the capital. This was the place where all such claims and actions had to be tested.

In some ways, the points of controversy in Jerusalem would be different from those in Galilee. Galilee was 'border country', on the frontier with pagan neighbours. So the central issues were all bound up with Jewish identity: What made a Jew a Jew? How could faithful Jews define themselves against their pagan neighbours and not compromise their religion? Hence all the disputes about the Sabbath, the food laws and the regulations about ritual purity.

Previous pages: **Aerial view of Jerusalem's Old City, where Jesus spent his last days, with the Kidron valley and the Judean desert beyond.**

In Jerusalem, the situation was different – it all had to do with Israel's history and destiny. Who was the true king? When would David's throne be restored? How could Yahweh be worshipped appropriately in a temple rebuilt by a non-Jew, Herod the Great? When would the pagan overlords be banished? When would the nations come up to Jerusalem as worshippers, to recognize the true God of Israel?

But there were ample signs already that Jesus had these questions firmly in his sights. He had already compared himself to King David. He had commended a Roman centurion for his faith, and spoken about 'many from the east and west' coming together into the kingdom. He had announced the 'acceptable year of the Lord' when God would do a new thing for his people. Jesus' agenda could not suddenly stop short of Jerusalem. It was its obvious destination. The only question was: when?

We sense the importance of this question in John's account. Jesus' brothers ask him if he is going up for the Feast of Tabernacles (normally in October). Jesus cryptically replies: 'My hour has not yet come' (John 7:8). In fact, Jesus does go up, but on his own and somewhat secretly. It would be a brief foray before a more climactic visit. This and other passages in John's Gospel make it clear that Jesus' ministry in fact involved several visits to Jerusalem – as indeed we might expect. The other Gospel writers, however, structure their account in such a way as to focus on Jesus' last and greatest visit to the city – when matters came to a head. For there was a true sense in which any previous visits to Jerusalem paled into insignificance when compared with this. They were preliminary skirmishes before the real battle. The question was: when would Jesus finally make the all-important bid?

The hour came in the third springtime of Jesus' public ministry. Now was the time, Jesus declared, to march upon the city. Speaking to his close followers near Caesarea

Philippi, he announced the shape of the journey to come. The 'Son of man' was going up to Jerusalem; there would be conflict, even death, but he would be vindicated and glorified. It would be tough for his followers; but if they were up for it, if they too were willing to 'take up their crosses', then it was time to be setting off.

The idea that Jesus would suffer in making his messianic bid was a chilling one; Peter protested against this part of the script. But, in general terms, this was exciting stuff – it was the news they had all been secretly waiting for. After Jesus had fed the 5,000, the crowds had wanted to make him king but he had withdrawn to the hills (John 6:15). This time, however, the royal candidate announced at last the launch of his campaign. The revolution of the kingdom was beginning: from that time on, Jesus 'set his face to go to Jerusalem' (Luke 9:51). Jesus knew what he was about: the disciples thought they did, but they did not.

'He then began to teach them that the Son of man must suffer many things and be rejected by the elders, chief priests and teachers of the law, and that he must be killed and after three days rise again.'

MARK 8:31

The reasons for the journey

Jesus' followers and the pilgrim crowds gathering on the road up to Jerusalem may have had all kinds of agendas of their own, but what was in Jesus' own mind? After all, if he had wanted a quiet life, it would have been far better to remain in Galilee, preaching about God's mercy and love. But Jesus' message was far more than that, and he simply could not stay. He deliberately entered into the storm clouds which hung over Jerusalem.

On the surface of things, he was simply going up to Jerusalem, as were vast numbers of his fellow Galileans, to celebrate Passover. This in itself gives us an important clue as to Jesus' special purposes in making this journey. If Jesus had a message of 'liberty for the captives' (Luke 4:18), if Jesus saw it as his mission in life to bring about a long-awaited freedom, then he could not pass by for ever the opportunity of a Passover weekend in Jerusalem. For this was the festival that focused on precisely that hope – God's deliverance.

The critic of the nation

But there were other reasons for setting out for Jerusalem. For a start, Jesus was being heralded by the people as a prophet. After four centuries of comparative silence on God's part, people were again hearing the 'word of the Lord' – first from John the Baptist, and now from Jesus. Jesus was being compared to Elijah and Jeremiah. No lesser category would account for the sheer power of this man, combined with the authority of his teaching. Indeed the ultimate comparison was perhaps with Moses himself. For in their scriptures, Jesus' contemporaries read of Moses' promise that God would eventually send another 'prophet like me' (Deuteronomy 18:14–22).

Passover in Judaism

Passover was one of the central festivals within the life of Israel. In the book of Exodus, the Israelites were commanded to cover their door lintels with the blood of a lamb. The angel of death, sent by God to bring death to all the first-born of Egypt, would then 'pass over' their homes. It was the prelude to their miraculous escape from Pharaoh and their journey from slavery to the promised land.

Participants remembered the events in a profound way, seeing themselves as actually among those who were rescued from Egypt. The festival was an annual reminder of God's mercy but also an opportunity to pray for a new act of deliverance. For Pharaoh had simply been replaced by other pagan rulers – most recently the Roman Caesar. The Roman garrison (the 'Antonia Fortress') looked out ominously over their temple courts. So they were hoping for a new exodus and a new freedom.

Pilgrims came up to Jerusalem for the festival from all over the Diaspora and especially from Galilee. The number of people in Jerusalem would swell from around 120,000 to anything up to 500,000.

But no prophet of this stature could stay on the sidelines in Galilee. Prophets traditionally brought their powerful words to be heard by the rulers at the heart of the nation – frequently at great personal risk. Jesus could not make his solemn warnings from a safe hideout in the north. True prophets had to act on the truth of their own words and speak them where they might cause offence.

Already, in Galilee, Jesus had given clear hints that he had a tough message for the Israel of his day, focused on its leadership in Jerusalem. Those who had come down from Jerusalem to investigate him had been told in no uncertain terms that when they likened him to the 'prince of demons' they were in danger of committing an

Jews flock to the Jerusalem temple for the annual Passover festival, where they are overlooked by the Roman Antonia Fortress. Watercolour by Peter Connolly (b. 1935).

'O Jerusalem, Jerusalem, you who kill the prophets and stone those sent to you, how often I have longed to gather your children together, as a hen gathers her chicks under her wings, but you were not willing! Look, your house is left to you desolate.'

LUKE 13:34–35

unforgivable sin (Mark 3:29). Villages in Galilee that failed to respond appropriately to Jesus were denounced by him in terms reminiscent of the prophets' words against Babylon. Jerusalem must have its moment of reckoning as well. Overhanging all Jesus' ministry was this note of warning and threat. Great tribulation awaited 'this generation'; Jerusalem's 'house' (the temple) would become 'desolate' and the 'house built on sand' would crash (Luke 13:35; Matthew 7:26–27). Like Jeremiah, Jesus had a strong message of warning for the city. But it could not be delivered by someone else. He had to go there in person.

The challenge to the temple

But Jerusalem was not just the central headquarters of Israel's leadership. It was first and foremost a city centred around the temple. This was the place where God's Name and his special presence was believed to dwell, and the divinely appointed place for receiving his forgiveness through sacrifice. But now Jesus was doing things that invited comparison with the temple, and even in some ways challenged it.

Jesus' provocative act in telling a paralytic man that he had 'authority to forgive sins' (Mark 2:1–12) was a deliberate challenge to a worldview focused around the temple. Was this not Jesus claiming to do what God alone could do? And if divine forgiveness was now possible without the temple sacrifices, what sacrifice was Jesus going to offer in their place? But Jesus had done more than this. He had made his challenge explicit. 'One greater than the temple is here,' he claimed, 'one greater even than Solomon', the builder of the original temple (Matthew 12:6, 42). And if the temple was the place that spoke of God's presence among his people, then people were beginning to sense that in Jesus, too, they were finding that presence. He was, as it were, a one man counter-temple movement, embodying in his own person that which had previously been focused on the temple –

God's own presence and God's great forgiveness. He was the place where the living God was at work to heal, restore and regroup his people. So Jesus constituted a challenge to all the temple stood for. Going up to Jerusalem, he would undoubtedly head straight to the temple.

The claimant to the throne

Jesus' claims, however, were not just to do with being a prophet or a challenge to the temple. He was also a messianic claimant. The Messiah (among other things) was the 'son of David' who was entitled to royal acclaim in Jerusalem. Sooner or later any royal claimant must go to the capital to press his claim. Jesus' whole message was focused on the 'kingdom of God', but Jerusalem was the place where God had to be re-encountered as king of his people. If God was now becoming king, if Jesus was himself identifying himself as the agent of God's kingly rule, then this king sooner or later had to come to his capital city.

So, there were many reasons why Jesus set out on his historic journey. The man who promised freedom must go up to join in the Passover's celebrations; the prophet had to speak to the nation's leaders; the one challenging the monopoly of the temple had to enter its courts; the messianic claimant had to enter the capital. But running beneath all of these purposes there lay another, darker strand. It was the most important reason of them all. For Jesus was also going to Jerusalem to die.

The crossroad

At a purely pragmatic level, it is not hard to imagine that a person coming to Jerusalem embodying all these hopes and claims would almost certainly end up in trouble. After all, there were a lot of vested interests in the city that would not look kindly upon being challenged by this Galilean upstart. And Jesus showed no signs of taking an alternative route. But did Jesus actively intend to die?

We have already seen how one of the concepts Jesus

used to explain his mission was the 'suffering servant' found in Isaiah. Another concept available to him was that of the 'messianic woes'. This was the belief that the longed-for age of the Messiah would only come about after a time of testing and trial for Israel. Within this world of ideas it becomes somewhat easier to understand how Jesus might well have seen his death as an essential part of his vocation. Perhaps, after all, this was the only way in which the messianic age could be introduced. Perhaps he was called to be that 'suffering servant'. If, as Messiah, he embodied the hopes and destiny of Israel as a whole, then maybe he himself would have to go through that time of severe testing and trial on behalf of Israel.

'The Son of man... came to serve, and to give his life as a ransom for many.'

MARK 10:45

Even so, this idea of the Messiah being the suffering servant was a radical new twist in the story. The Messiah was supposed to get rid of the Romans, not end up being killed by them.

'The days will come when the bridegroom is taken away.'

MARK 2:20

But Jesus had made this clear to his disciples on several occasions. The shadow of the cross went a long way back into his ministry. And, once he arrived in Jerusalem, this would become even clearer. The 'beloved son' in the parable of the vineyard would not be welcomed but would be cast out and killed (Mark 14:8). Alluding to the 'suffering servant' passages in Isaiah, he would explain: 'It is written, "And he was numbered with the transgressors"; and I tell you that this must be fulfilled in me' (Luke 22:37). Jesus clearly saw himself as the servant who would die.

So Jesus set out for Jerusalem with much on his mind, with much to accomplish. Luke refers in fact to his need to bring about a 'new exodus', a new act of God bringing liberation to his people (Luke 9:31). So this was going to be a Passover with a difference – indeed a new Passover with a whole new meaning.

From Caesarea Philippi to Jericho

Jesus and the disciples travelled from the region of Caesarea Philippi, the scene of the transfiguration, down to Lake Galilee and then on towards Jericho. Only after that would they begin to climb again – this time through the barren hills of the Judean desert.

It was a journey the disciples would never forget. Jesus used it as an opportunity to teach his close disciples more of what it would mean to follow in his way. Luke in his account devotes a third of his entire Gospel to this 'travel narrative', giving the sense that much of Jesus' ministry was conducted 'on the move' with Jesus' sights firmly set on Jerusalem.

'I must keep going... for surely no prophet can die outside Jerusalem!'
LUKE 13:33

The disciples are rebuked for their debates about 'who is the greatest' and their hopes of getting the best seats next to Jesus when he becomes king. Picking up a small child, Jesus warns them that the 'kingdom of God belongs to such as these'. In a similar vein, he warns a rich young ruler that his reliance on his wealth is acting as a block to his enjoyment of God's kingdom. But when a blind beggar called Bartimaeus exercises persistent faith in Jesus, he is healed and joins others in 'following Jesus along the road'.

The news that Jesus was on the move, heading for Jerusalem, evidently went ahead of him and caused a stir of excitement. The hot streets in the oasis-town of Jericho began to fill up with crowds as word got round that Jesus was about to pass through. Zacchaeus, an unpopular tax collector, climbed a tree to ensure a good view. But he got more than he bargained for. Jesus spotted him, ruined his

Jericho, the city of palms, is the oldest city in the world, located some 300 metres (nearly 1,000 feet) below sea level in the Jordan valley.

own reputation (once again) by asking to go to his house, and then went on his way having announced that Zacchaeus had been restored to the company of God's true people – all because of his response to Jesus. It was a brilliant way for Jesus to make his subversive point: 'The Son of man came to seek and to save what was lost' (Luke 19:10).

From Jericho to Jerusalem

So Jesus left Jericho with expectations running rife about what would happen next. The start of his final ascent up to Jerusalem caused people, we read, to think that the 'kingdom of God was going to appear at once' (Luke 19:11). This captures for us in a nutshell the mood of the times and the longings of Jesus' contemporaries. They longed to see their God become king; they longed for the Romans to be ousted; they longed for a leader who would implement God's new order. So when Jesus set off through the desert, all kinds of bells were ringing in their minds.

Wadi Qelt in the Judean desert, one of the valleys going up from Jericho towards Jerusalem.

After all, it was through a 'desert' that God long ago had brought his people into the promised land. Was the same pattern about to repeat itself? Isaiah (40:3ff.) had prophesied that a highway for God himself would be blazed through the desert so that the Holy One of Israel could begin his mighty work of restoration. This was the desert frequented by John the Baptist and the Essene community, both with their vision of what God would do for Israel. The desert might be a lonely place, but it certainly had powerful connections in the Jewish mind.

Into this situation, awash with expectation, Jesus told one of his most distinctive parables (Luke 19:11–27). Jesus' parables were designed to get people to view things in new ways. The parable of the 10 'minas' certainly does that. At this distance in time, however, we cannot be sure we have correctly grasped Jesus' intended meaning.

The story was based on a recent event, known very well to Jesus' audience: after the death of his father, Herod the Great, the young Archelaus had gone off to Rome, in order to have his claim to the throne confirmed. While he was away, however, people had rebelled against him. So Jesus begins: 'A man of noble birth went to a distant country to have himself appointed king and then to return.' Was Jesus about to hint at the end of Roman rule in Jerusalem? In Jesus' subversive retelling of the story, however, the returning king is not deposed, but instead metes out punishment on the rebels. It is those who had soundly invested the king's money (their 10 minas), who are praised. This is hardly the kind of thing the populace wanted to hear. The story has been twisted in a disturbing new direction.

'They were on their way up to Jerusalem, with Jesus leading the way, and the disciples were astonished, while those who followed were afraid.'

MARK 10:32

But who, then, is this king? As so often in Jesus' parables, the first presumption is that he has taken an episode from human life and is using it to talk about God – the ultimate king. But there is also a hint here that Jesus is using this story to talk about himself and to explain his own actions. It is not surprising, then, that this parable has often been taken as a reference to Jesus' own return at some future date. Jesus would then be calling his followers to be faithful in the meantime until he returns. If so, this would then be Jesus' way of dampening down the false excitement of the Jericho crowds – the kingdom of God will not be fully implemented for a long, long time. Yet, however true this may be when applied as a pattern for the church, it is far more likely that Jesus was saying something that was even more directly relevant to his actual hearers.

All becomes clear when we begin to see that Jesus is indeed the king in the parable, but the 'return' of the king is to be identified with *Jesus' imminent arrival in Jerusalem*. Jesus is then warning his hearers that the appearance of the kingdom, which they rightly expect to occur when he gets to Jerusalem, is not going to be a straightforward matter for rejoicing. Instead it will be a moment of judgment for any who do not wish King Jesus to rule over them.

Jesus is making a devastating claim for himself. For if Jesus is talking of himself as the king, why does he talk of himself as 'returning'? Has he been there at some point in the distant past? Suddenly we hear again the prophetic hope in Isaiah that one day Yahweh, the Lord himself, would 'return to Zion' (Isaiah 52:8). Yahweh was the true king of Zion/Jerusalem who had departed at the time of the exile. Now he is returning, declares Jesus, – and he is doing so in and as me. Watch my entrance into Jerusalem. For in that event, you will be witnessing the long-awaited 'return of the Lord' to Zion.

'Blessed is the king who comes in the name of the Lord!'

LUKE 19:38

It is a mind-blowing claim. Jesus goes up to Jerusalem not just as prophet, Messiah and servant; he goes up embodying the purposes and the person of the Lord himself.

***The life of Jesus*: Jericho to the Mount of Olives**

Leaving Jericho, Jesus and his companions would have had a steep climb on their way up to Jerusalem. The desert would have been slightly green at this time of year, with some scant vegetation, but it was an inhospitable part if one needed to spend a night in it. Jesus knew this desert well from his 40 days of 'testing' at the outset of his ministry. Now it was a time of even greater testing.

As he begins his final climb up the back of the Mount of Olives and sees the welcome lights of Bethany to his left, one senses that the time has now come for a showdown. The long journey from Galilee, planned long ago, will soon be over, but the real drama is only just about to begin. These last hours in the desert are 'the calm before the storm'.

So Jesus had a distinct agenda and an awesome destiny. This was a man with a mission, bent upon reaching his goal. This was someone with a unique sense of his own identity – an identity which he could only hint at in prophetic riddles and which, in the short term, would not lead to his own glory. This was someone who knew his darkest hour lay just ahead, that opposition was inevitable, and that he would need to draw upon the deepest resources of his personality for faith and stamina. This was a king about to be rejected by his own.

CHAPTER 9

Arrival in the City

Jesus at last reaches the outskirts of Jerusalem. It is the beginning of one of the most famous and well-documented weeks in ancient history. The Synoptic writers (especially Luke) give the impression that Jesus went straight over the Mount of Olives and down into the city. His arrival is portrayed as the direct culmination of the long journey begun in Galilee. But this may be a telescoped account. Instead (as suggested by John) Jesus probably detoured first to Bethany.

Overnight in Bethany

Jesus arrived in Bethany 'six days before the Passover' (John 12:1), knowing that here at least he could be assured of a positive reception. It was the home of his friends, Mary and Martha, and their brother Lazarus, whom Jesus had raised from the dead during a previous visit (John 11). This act that had sent shock waves back into the city. 'It could well be expedient', Caiaphas the high priest had suggested, 'that this one man should die' – an ironic fate for a man with power to bring others to life. Even so, this home would provide a welcome break from the storm, both now and in the coming days – a haven for Jesus and his disciples in the midst of a dangerous enterprise, a base camp from which they could make 'sorties' into Jerusalem.

And it was here in Bethany, at a neighbouring house belonging to 'Simon the Leper', that Jesus would be on the receiving end of one of the most thoughtful deeds of his life (Mark 14:3–11). Mary, also known as Mary Magdalene, entered with

The Passion narratives

The early Christians ascribed great significance to Jesus' death. In addition to some references in the book of Hebrews to Gethsemane and Golgotha (5:7; 13:12), the four Gospels each give a large proportion of their account to the 'Passion narratives', which describe Jesus' last days. Mark's Gospel has been called a 'Passion narrative with an extended introduction'.

Matthew's account is very similar to Mark's. John's account gives a different perspective (with five chapters focused exclusively on Jesus' Last Supper with his disciples, and greater detail in the trial before Pilate). Luke emphasizes the significance of Jesus' arrival for the fate of Jerusalem and shows how Jesus was innocent of the political charges brought against him.

Nineteenth-century photo of Bethany, the last outpost before the desert.

some expensive ointment and anointed Jesus' feet. It was a powerful prophetic act, betraying her fearful intuition as to what awaited Jesus: he was soon to be anointed for burial. Mary was determined to show her impulsive devotion – before it was too late. Others looking on were appalled: it was not just unseemly, but grossly extravagant. But Jesus knew what she meant: 'The poor will always be with you; you will not always have me.' Mary knew what Jesus knew – that this time his coming to Jerusalem would end not in life but in death.

This then sets the tone for all that happens next. Events in Bethany send out a dramatic and seemingly contradictory signal. This Jesus, who in raising Lazarus had shown his power over death, is himself actively embracing his own imminent death.

And something was also stirring in the heart of one of his close friends. Judas Iscariot, the disciple in charge of the group's finances, complained at Mary's waste of money. Maybe Jesus' stern reply, betraying Jesus' seeming acceptance of his death, tipped the balance for Judas. If that was what the Master wanted, then he could have it.

This alabaster perfume juglet from the 10th century BC may be reminiscent of the one that Mary Magdalene used when she anointed Jesus.

'The great crowd that had come to the festival heard that Jesus was coming to Jerusalem. So they took branches of palm trees and went out to meet him.'

JOHN 12:12–13

The entrance into Jerusalem

The next day dawned. It was time for the first sortie into Jerusalem. It would take about 45 minutes to walk into the city. There was still a real sense of climax for those in Jesus' retinue, about to get their first glimpse of the 'holy city'. Halting in Bethany, however, also allowed more time for the news to spread that the Galilean preacher was coming up to the festival – locals could get ready to greet him.

Jesus clearly had his own agenda for the day as well. He had been waiting for this moment, and he had made some plans. He wanted to use this warm reception to make a point. He told his disciples to go and fetch a young donkey from the nearby hamlet of Bethphage, because 'the Lord had need of it'.

A prophecy in Israel's scriptures spoke of Jerusalem's king entering the city 'humble and riding on a donkey'

'Rejoice greatly, O daughter Zion!... Lo, your king comes to you; triumphant and victorious is he, humble and riding on a donkey.'

ZECHARIAH 9:9

Christ's Entry into Jerusalem **by Sergijewski Possad (15th century).**

(Zechariah 9:9). The donkey was a sign. Jesus wanted the Jerusalem crowds to have a far deeper cause for rejoicing: they were not just welcoming a controversial prophet from backwater Galilee, they were in fact welcoming their 'king'. As we have seen before, the true king of Jerusalem was not just the Messiah, but also in a profound sense Yahweh himself. God had always been the city's true king, and the prophets longed for this king, their God, to return and take up his residence there. Now, in a way they could not have imagined, he was coming – seated on a young donkey. It was a staggering implication. No wonder Jesus let people cry out: 'Blessed is the king who comes in the name of the Lord!' No wonder he told the Pharisees that, if the crowds were hushed up, then 'the very stones would cry out'. This was the city's finest hour – the 'city of the Great King' welcoming that divine king.

The discordant note

In the midst of the celebration, however, the one at its very centre began to weep. It was the painful irony that broke Jesus' heart. The crowds were welcoming him but they did not know what they were doing – nor what lay in store for him. Jerusalem was bedecked in all its festive finery, but Jesus the prophet could see how it would look when it was destroyed within a generation.

Jerusalem, the so-called 'city of peace', was going the way of war. It was foolishly girding up its strength in opposition to mighty Rome. And it would not win. And somehow that tragic event was bound up in the purposes of God with this strange event that was happening right now – the arrival of the city's true king. There was a vital link between them. Just as the glitter of his own reception would evaporate into indifference and hostility, so too the glory of Jerusalem would disappear in a mess of fire and fury. And the former tragedy would be connected to the latter one. If it was a great moment for Jerusalem to be receiving her king, it would be a tragic moment when she rejected him. So Jesus wept. He had wept before – in Bethany with the mourners for Lazarus. Now he wept again, this time on his own, for the future of Jerusalem, the city he had always loved.

'As he came near and saw the city, he wept over it, saying, "If you, even you, had only recognized on this day the things that make for peace! But now they are hidden from your eyes. Indeed, the days will come… when your enemies will… surround you… They will crush you to the ground… and they will not leave one stone upon another; because you did not recognize the time of your visitation from God."'

LUKE 19:41–44

The humble king

As a bare historical event, Jesus' entry into Jerusalem probably occupied very little time. The time span from the moment when the crowds burst into praise at the place where 'the road goes down the Mount of Olives' (Luke 19:37) to the moment when Jesus entered the eastern gate of the city, might have been no more than

15 minutes. We do not hear of the Roman authorities coming out to check the situation. Almost certainly, this popular demonstration would have been well over before the troops needed to dispel the crowd – if indeed that was necessary anyway. Jesus' action, though clearly messianic and provocative in that sense, was also clearly non-aggressive. In contrast to other messianic figures in subsequent years who would storm Jerusalem on horseback, Jesus' donkey parodied any such military intentions. Both his fellow Jews and the Romans could detect that this Messiah was not going to be fighting Rome. He came in peace, not war. He was a king with a different kind of kingdom. It was a brief prophetic act, scarcely understood in the few moments of its happening, but which would later speak powerfully of Jesus' distinctive personal agenda.

Jesus himself drew this powerful scene to a close. This was his moment of triumph, as he was swept up on a tide of popular acclaim through the capital's gates. But instead of seizing the moment, he deliberately defused the situation. He went as expected into the temple, but (contrary to Luke's telescoped account) we learn that he simply 'looked around at everything' and then returned to Bethany (Mark 11:11). It was quite an anticlimax.

The next day in the temple

This was all a necessary part of Jesus' distinctive messianic approach. He would be giving messianic hints during his stay in Jerusalem, but they would be deliberately cut short to prevent the crowds having the time to misconstrue things in line with their alternative, more political agenda. The same would be true for the next sortie. This time Jesus would indeed do something memorable in the temple.

As noted before, one of the expected roles for the Messiah was that he would restore the temple to its former glory after the setbacks of the exile. Ever since the days of Solomon, royalty and temple had gone together hand in hand. This was perhaps why Herod the Great had rebuilt the temple – all part of his bid to be recognized as the true king. So Jesus entered the temple once more. But this time he did more than look around. He caused an almighty stir, overturning the tables of the money changers. In contemporary practice, those offering sacrifices were required to purchase their sacrificial animals using a special temple currency. So, in interrupting the work of the money changers, Jesus was effectively preventing people from offering their sacrifices. In later terminology, this was his 'cleansing of the temple'.

This single event has attracted more scholarly attention in recent years than any other in Jesus' ministry. For it takes us to the very heart of Jesus' agenda, as well as providing the most likely trigger for the events leading up to his arrest. This episode finally made it clear to the

Aerial view (looking northwards) of the Jerusalem temple platform, with the recent excavations to its south and west.

authorities that there would be no peace until this Jesus had somehow been removed. And it immediately provoked the question of Jesus' authority: 'By what authority are you doing these things?' (Mark 11:28). Given the link (noted above) between the Messiah and the temple, we sense just how important this question was.

A portent of destruction?

But what, more precisely, was Jesus seeking to say about the temple by this provocative action? It was clearly vitally important within his mission. Why else would he bring himself into such disrepute if the issues were not essential?

Seen in this light, some of the popular explanations appear somewhat thin. Was Jesus really just objecting to a recent ruling that traders could occupy the outer court, the Court of the Gentiles? There is no doubt that Jesus did

Archaeology of the temple

Herod the Great began rebuilding the Jewish temple on the ancient site of Solomon's temple in 19 BC. He extended the platform considerably to the south, making space for the Court of the Gentiles, in which Jesus found the money changers. Moving northwards, was then a low fence through which only Jews could pass. At the centre was an empty shrine, the Holy of Holies – almost certainly now covered by the structures of the Muslim Dome of the Rock.

The rebuilding work was only just complete when the temple was destroyed by Titus in August AD 70. Some of Herod's massive stones, which were 'thrown down' in keeping with Jesus' prediction (Mark 13:2), can still be seen at the south-western corner where they landed on the shops and pavements below.

'He began driving out those who were buying and selling there. He overturned the tables of the money changers... He said, "Is it not written: 'My house will be called a house of prayer for all nations'? But you have made it 'a den of robbers'."'

MARK 11:15, 17

object to this. After all, it made it impossible for Gentiles to experience the temple as a 'house of prayer for all nations'. But is that all? Would Jesus have been content if the traders had simply moved elsewhere? If that is indeed all he wanted, then he seems clearly not to have achieved this (quite limited) goal. For almost certainly, 'normal service' was resumed within a matter of 30 minutes or so. The tables were soon put back in place.

No, we are dealing here with a brief prophetic act, neither long enough to worry the Romans, nor orchestrated enough to excite the populace to join in. Jesus is a solitary figure, performing his own singular act.

Far more likely, then, is the argument that Jesus intended this brief action to be symbolic of something larger. It was, as the textbooks call it, a 'portent of destruction'. Jesus overturned the tables (and symbolically interrupted the very process that was necessary for the conducting of the temple sacrifices) to signal that the temple was under divine judgment and in imminent danger of being brought to an end. Jesus himself, of course, could not single-handedly bring about the end of the temple, but he could hint at it in this powerful prophetic way.

Confirmation of this more radical explanation comes in several places. Mark in his Gospel, for example, deliberately sandwiches his account of this temple episode between the two-part story of Jesus cursing the fig tree. Jesus had approached a fig tree on the way in from Bethany and cursed it for being without fruit – even though it was not the season for figs. The next morning the disciples passed it again and noticed it had 'withered from the roots'. Mark wants us to see this otherwise senseless act of destruction as a parallel act which Jesus was using to explain what he was doing in the temple. The disciples are let in on the secret that Jesus was cursing the temple because it was failing to produce the fruit that God required. And, just as the fig tree withered, so now in due course would the temple be brought to an end.

'"My house will be called a house of prayer." But you have made it "a den of robbers".' *Christ Driving the Money Changers Out of the Temple* by Carl Heinrich Bloch (1834–90).

Moreover, all the Synoptic Gospels portray Jesus as having a private conversation with his disciples soon after this in which he expressly predicts of the temple that 'not one stone will be left upon another' (Mark 13:2) – the very same phrase he had used when weeping over the city the day before. Jesus evidently believed that the days of this great temple were numbered, and he conveyed this in public and in private, in words and in deed. The public act was necessarily more ambiguous – which is why the authorities came back to question him – but, taken as a whole, the message was clear. Truly, for this great Herodian temple the end was nigh.

Such a message would not, of course, be popular with those with vested interests in the temple – the high priests, the Sadducees, and indeed any who liked the status quo. However, those who were more critical of the temple (such as the Essenes or some of the Pharisees) might respond to

Jesus' action more positively. But if so, then they would be expecting this current temple to be replaced by another, truly 'restored' temple. If that is what Jesus was pointing to, all well and good. Some scholars think Jesus was indeed predicting just such a new 'bricks and mortar' temple. But the evidence suggests Jesus saw things differently. Yes, he would build a replacement temple, but of a completely different kind.

The replacement temple

We learn this from noting a strange feature, brought up later at Jesus' trial before the high priest. His opponents on that occasion would try to reconstruct the exact wording of another cryptic remark made by Jesus about the temple's destruction. The correct wording is probably recorded in John's Gospel: 'Destroy this temple, and I will raise it again in three days' (John 2:19). This cryptic remark contains an awesome truth, grasped later by his followers because of another event that took place 'after three days': Jesus saw himself as the new restored temple. We have noted Jesus' actions and statements, beginning in Galilee, in which he was issuing a challenge to the temple's monopoly as the sole place of divine forgiveness and presence. Now in Jerusalem, he pushed that claim to its logical conclusion: he himself was the true temple.

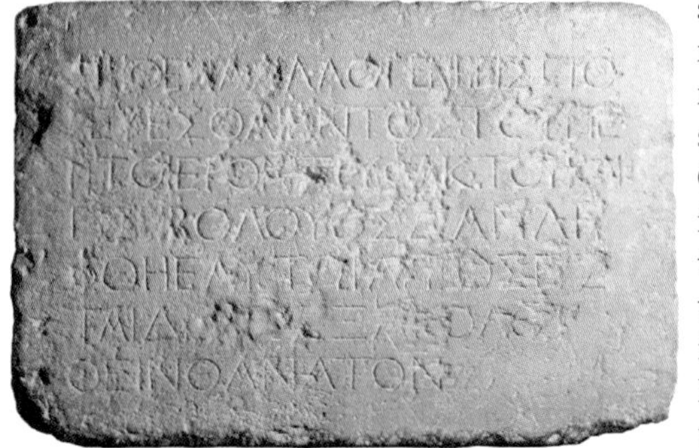

On this stone, there is a warning to Gentiles not to trespass into the temple's inner courts, upon pain of death.

So the reasons why the temple was soon to be eclipsed were many-layered. There were, no doubt, specific abuses – of which this latest episode with the traders was but the latest. The temple was also in danger of losing its religious function and becoming instead a political symbol, a rallying point and focus for the growing national movement of resistance against Rome. Jesus' critique was not without substance or cause. But beneath these surface issues there was something deeper at work. God's purposes were beginning to enter a new phase. The temple, God-ordained as it was, was embodying certain truths which Jesus knew would soon be redundant – its strict distinction between Jew and Gentile, its claim to manifest the presence of Israel's God, its assertion that this was the only place where sacrifices could atone for sins. For into the midst of Israel's life had come a person, a presence – a sacrificial victim – who would expose God's purposes to the whole world. The time had come for the temple's demise, because the time had come for the world's redemption.

Jesus' short-lived act thus had vast meaning and enormous consequences. He was not just overturning a few tables. He was overturning centuries of expectation, and laying a piece of dynamite at the root of Israel's central institution. Even if not all the implications were clear at once, enough was clear for the authorities to take due note. This strange Galilean prophet could not be right; he must be wrong. And, if wrong, he was clearly dangerous, likely to lead Israel astray and, worse still, a nuisance and a menace in Jerusalem's delicate political stand-off with Rome. Jesus had implied that it was only a matter of time before the temple came crashing down; the authorities replied that it was only a matter of time before this Jesus was himself to be put down. The battle lines were being drawn.

Debates in the temple courts

As far as we can tell, Jesus spent the next few days commuting in from Bethany to the temple. The slopes of the Mount of Olives would by now have been covered with tents as more and more Galileans arrived and set up camp for the celebration of Passover. On some nights, Jesus' party may have done the same, but Matthew's account (21:17) suggests that they took advantage of a roof over their heads in Bethany. After all, it was only a further 20 minutes' walk beyond the crest of the Mount but just

'Each day Jesus was teaching at the temple, and each evening he went out to spend the night on the hill called the Mount of Olives.'

LUKE 21:37

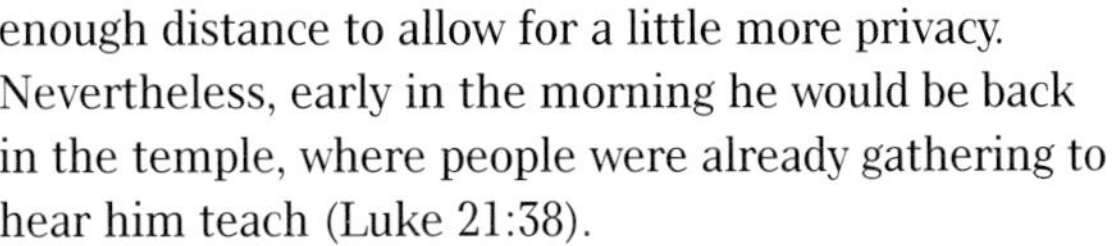

enough distance to allow for a little more privacy. Nevertheless, early in the morning he would be back in the temple, where people were already gathering to hear him teach (Luke 21:38).

According to Mark, the very next day after his overturning of the tables, Jesus was indeed back in the temple, being tested with a series of questions (Mark 11:27 – 12:40): 'By what authority' had he cleansed the temple? 'Is it right to pay taxes to Caesar or not?' Did he believe in the resurrection of the dead? 'Which is the most important commandment?' These were key questions asked of a key person at a critical time. Some people were genuinely trying to make him out, others to trip him up. Would he side with the Romans or the revolutionaries, with the Pharisees or the Sadducees? Would he put a foot wrong when discussing the Law? Jesus cut his own line through this veritable minefield, leaving many of the questioners nonplussed, amazed or embarrassed.

Coin from the reign of Caesar Augustus, with an image of the emperor.

Jesus also had some questions of his own: If you now accept the ministry of John the Baptist as a prophet, why do you not accept me? Why do you argue about paying tribute to Caesar, when you are failing to give your own God his dues? How come you theologians seem to know 'neither the scriptures nor the power of God'? Why do people come up with rude excuses when God has a banquet waiting for them? Why did David seem to call the Messiah his 'Lord' (as in Psalm 110)? And, most pointedly, what do you think the tenants in the vineyard (a well-known metaphor for Israel) will do if ever the owner (Israel's God) sends his 'beloved son' to collect some of his rightful fruit? What if the tenants reject and kill him? Will not God vindicate his son and turn the vineyard over to others?

People were challenging Jesus, but he in return was laying down the gauntlet. It was the necessary contest of words in public before the battle shifted to another, more secret, arena. Jesus was not making it easy for his opponents. Courageously and blatantly he was standing 'daily' in the temple courts, making plain his claims for himself and his prophetic critique of others.

Matthew summarizes some of Jesus' teaching in a devastating chapter consisting of seven 'woes' pronounced on the 'teachers of the Law and the Pharisees' (chapter 23). Itemizing different aspects of their practice he describes them as 'blind guides' and 'hypocrites'. At the same time, he insists that his followers should 'obey everything they tell you', but 'do not do what they do'. It is a powerful challenge, as Jesus lays down his alternative vision for what constitutes true obedience to the Law. It is not a matter of lip service, but of obedience coming from the heart. Speaking in the centre of Israel's religious life, in the very same building where once as a boy of 12 he had himself learnt and discussed the meaning of the Law, he now urges Israel to follow his own alternative path. This Galilean prophet certainly did not shy away from outspokenness when once he hit the big city. No, it provoked him all the more and drew matters to a head.

Mysteries on the Mount of Olives

But there were some things which, though equally true, were better said in private. One day during that week, as he was leaving the temple, Jesus spoke again to his disciples about the temple's forthcoming destruction. Then he took his disciples on a short walk up the Mount of Olives to a quiet place where, overlooking the Temple Mount, they could continue their conversation alone. Peter, James, John and Andrew asked him when this event would take place.

Jesus' reply is known as the 'apocalyptic discourse' (Mark 13 and parallels). This is because it appears to move on from talking about the predicted destruction of the temple to other 'apocalyptic' events associated with the 'coming of the Son of man'. This 'coming' is then normally taken as a reference to 'the Second Coming' (the time of Jesus' return at some point in the future); however, it could refer instead to that moment when Jesus is finally vindicated as a true prophet (when his prediction about the temple came true in AD 70). In any event, Jesus warns that an unparalleled time of distress is coming; there will be 'wars and rumours of wars', Jesus' followers will be in particular trouble and those in Jerusalem will at some point need to 'flee to the mountains'. It will seem like the final End of the world – as indeed one would expect if the temple were destroyed – but in another sense this tragic event will itself be just a pointer to that End. For the fall of the temple will be a sign that in Jesus the end of the previous age has indeed occurred, and the new age of the kingdom has arrived – the 'age to come'. It will also be a sign, pointing forward to the ultimate End of all things when God's justice will be revealed to the entire world. So the most important thing that Jesus' disciples can do, rather than trying to use these few hints to second-guess the timing of these future events, is to ensure that they themselves are ready: 'Be on guard! Be alert! You do not know when that time will come… What I say to you, I say to everyone: "Watch!"'

'Heaven and earth will pass away, but my words will never pass away.'

MARK 13:31

***The life of Jesus*: Jerusalem's temple**

'Didn't you know that I had to be in my Father's house?' (Luke 2:49). Jesus, taken to the temple as an infant and again when aged 12, had the highest regard for the temple. So when he 'cleansed' the temple, it was inspired by the desire to correct abuses and by a 'zeal for God's house' (John 2:17). Yet he was also announcing his own authority over it and its forthcoming destruction.

Jesus' prophetic act triggered the events leading to his death. John's account, however, describes a temple cleansing at the outset of his ministry. John may have done this to express his conviction that Jesus was himself a new temple, the presence of God among us. Possibly, however, he is recording a separate episode, which Jesus then repeated on his final visit. This time, he did not get away with it.

Jesus' alternative vision

Sitting on the Mount of Olives, deliberately 'opposite' the temple (Mark 13:3), Jesus draws back the prophetic curtain – unveiling the future he sees for the temple, for Jerusalem, for his disciples and for the world. It must have been a chilling thing to hear. It was so contrary to what the disciples in their innocent earlier comments had been expecting to hear. For it revealed once again, only now more graphically, the alternative vision and agenda that lay behind all Jesus' words and deeds.

He did not see a bright prospect for Jerusalem, but dark clouds hovering in the wings. Yes, God's purposes would be worked out, but not in the expected ways. Being himself the 'Son of man', he – not Jerusalem, or even Israel – was at the centre of God's future plans. And it was his own followers – a small motley group now, but in due course including people from 'all nations' – who were truly God's 'elect' and chosen ones.

If he was right, then something enormous, without parallel thus far in the purposes of God, was about to be unveiled to an unsuspecting world. But, for that to come to pass, it was no use staying seated comfortably on the Mount of Olives enjoying the last days of Jerusalem's impressive panorama. He would have to go down into the valley, into the city and out the other side. If his vision of the future was to come to pass, there was a work to be done, one which he alone could do. It was time to go.

CHAPTER 10

Jesus' Last Hours

The drama comes to a climax on the Thursday evening. Jesus and the disciples are in a room in the upper city, celebrating Passover. It will prove a memorable occasion and the beginning of a long night.

The Passover with a difference

At the start of the meal, Jesus revealed the personal significance of this evening: 'I have eagerly desired to eat this Passover with you before I suffer' (Luke 22:15). It would be a last opportunity to be with his friends and to impart the essence of his teaching. This may explain why Jesus procured a private room in the upper city for the meal. He wanted them to be undisturbed, with time for one another, and space for truths to impress them deeply.

John's unhurried account (chapters 13–17) picks this up well, giving us an insight into the intimacy Jesus experienced with his close friends on this occasion. 'Having loved his own... he now showed them the full extent of his love' (John 13:1): he got down on his knees and started to wash their feet – the work of a servant. It also hinted at just how much he was about to do for them – hence what he would do a little later with the bread and wine.

The Passover, despite its focus on the past, was also fraught with future hopes as well – the longing that Israel's God would once again act to redeem his people from pagan slavery, that there would be a new exodus and an end to Israel's continued exile. No wonder the Roman troops were on red alert during the crowded Passover season in Jerusalem. The whole celebration was tinged with a note of frustration. It was in this context that Jesus celebrated his own passover meal and gave it a whole new meaning.

The new meaning

Following the pattern of the Passover liturgy, Jesus broke bread and lifted up a cup of wine, but he then said: 'This is my body given for you'; 'this is my blood, which is poured out for you'. Jesus had reworked the symbolism. The 'blood' they were giving thanks for was no longer that of the Passover lamb, but rather the blood of Jesus. Jesus had retold the story of Israel but had now placed his own story, his own death, in its centre. And the disciples found themselves invited to consume these strange gifts, knowing that they were thereby being drawn in some way into an acceptance of Jesus' imminent death.

No doubt they felt very uneasy at first. But they ate, and they drank. It was a critical moment in the life of Jesus, but also for his disciples. After all these years the shock waves of that powerful visual and dramatic act can still be felt. Two thousand years later, people are still breaking bread and drinking wine each week in remembrance.

It was in fact the third of Jesus' powerful 'prophetic acts' in Jerusalem: entering on a donkey, cleansing the temple, and now breaking bread (as a sign that his own

'This is my body given for you; do this in remembrance of me... This cup is the new covenant in my blood, which is poured out for you.'

LUKE 22:19, 20

Was the Last Supper a Passover meal?

The Passover meal always took place in the evening on the 15th day of the month called Nisan. The Synoptic Gospels give the impression that Jesus' Last Supper was indeed on Passover night (Mark 14:12). However, John's Gospel (13:1; 18:28; 19:31) might suggest it took place on the evening before the Passover (in other words, Nisan 14). Was Jesus perhaps following a different calendar (as used by the Pharisees or, more likely, the Essenes)?

But Jesus may simply have brought the meal forwards, knowing that 24 hours later he would be dead. Whatever the precise timing, Jesus intended this to be a meal that picked up the themes of Passover – as the Synoptic accounts bear witness.

body would soon be 'broken'). It also connected with those other two acts in powerful ways.

The temple would be destroyed, and the same would happen to Jesus – their fate was parallel and somehow interconnected. Jesus had hinted at the imminent end of the temple by overturning the tables, but now he was establishing a new, alternative table. In this way, he indicated that the place of God's presence was being relocated; he also revealed that one sacrificial system was being abolished because another was about to take its place – Jesus would give his own life for the sins of the world. And all this was taking place within the overarching context of a Messiah-figure entering Jerusalem, who yet

Early Christian wall painting from the catacomb of St Peter and Marcellinus, showing a eucharistic love feast – a communal meal commemorating the Last Supper.

was the divine king of Israel – God himself coming to do a new thing for his people, by bearing in his own person the consequences of the sins of his own people.

But all this meaning would have been lost if this meal had not been followed by Jesus' death. For the meal derived all its subsequent power and meaning from an event that at that precise moment was still to be accomplished. If the speaker meant what he said, he now had a horrific task to perform. No wonder the atmosphere was sorrowful that night, no wonder Jesus speaks frequently of his 'departure' that will cause them grief.

At some point in the proceedings, there is another departure. Jesus had already given the shocking news that one of the men around the table was a traitor. Now Judas leaves. It was only a short walk to the house of the high priest, and Judas was hoping to be paid some money for passing over some important information. Not only was the wanted man, Jesus, in a morbid frame of mind. He had also given, perhaps for the first time in recent days, a clear indication as to where he would be in a few hours' time. He would be in an olive grove called Gethsemane. If the high priest wanted to arrest him, this was his chance.

The ancient stepped street in Jerusalem, which Jesus may have used on his way down from the Last Supper to the Garden of Gethsemane.

The Garden of Gethsemane

Jesus and the disciples left the upper city a couple of hours later and walked up through the Kidron valley to the Garden of Gethsemane. It would take the best part of an hour to walk to this enclosed garden area at the foot of the Mount of Olives. Jesus withdrew a little from the main group, taking Peter, James and John with him; but they, too, were eventually left alone as Jesus prayed. One by one, the disciples fell asleep – even the three Jesus had asked to keep watch with him.

In that dark solitude, stripped of human support, surrounded only by olive trees, Jesus had to do business with God. He was standing on the threshold of a path that would lead inexorably to his death, a place to which he had deliberately brought himself. This was the 'hour of darkness'. He had committed himself in word and deed to this strange task; all the aspects of his ministry now focused on this lonely point and acted as a spur, prodding him to go forward. But it was one thing to speak of one's own death, even to break a piece of bread, but quite another to go through with it.

'My soul is overwhelmed with sorrow to the point of death. Stay here and keep watch with me.'

MATTHEW 26:38

'Father (Abba)... take this cup from me,' he cried, longing for there to be another way; 'yet not my will, but

'And being in anguish, he prayed more earnestly, and his sweat was like drops of blood falling to the ground.'

LUKE 22:44

yours be done.' That was the mark of resolve, the willing submission to God's call. In God's purposes, there was no other way – there was no avoiding the cross. And the imagery of the 'cup' picked up Old Testament images of God giving his enemies the cup of his wrath and judgment to drink. Jesus now resolved to take this 'cup' and to drink its fearful contents. Yet he needed to be sure that it came from none other than God himself. Jesus said he had come to 'give his life as a ransom for many' (Mark 10:45); now he determined to do exactly what he had promised. He would drink the cup of God's judgment and so bring life to others.

The choice of waiting

As any visitor to Jerusalem knows, Jesus could easily have continued up the Mount of Olives and had a bed for the night in Bethany. Instead he waited. Gethsemane reveals more than anything else the key element of Jesus' choice. He might look 'passive' enough in the events that would follow, dragged around at the will of others, but here he had an active choice. And he chose to wait.

'Unless an ear of wheat falls to the ground and dies, it remains only a single seed. But if it dies, it produces many seeds.'

JOHN 12:24

Gethsemane's location also makes clear in a graphic way the distinctive nature of Jesus' ministry. Consider the two options that we too are habitually presented with: fight or flight. Those options were there in Jesus' day too. The movement of national resistance would urge the former – a storming of Jerusalem in pursuit of freedom, forcing the hand of God. On the other hand, movements like the Essenes would take the other path, retreating into the quiet of the desert to await God's own intervention. Jesus took a middle path. Now that he had caused sufficient sensation in the capital, he could easily have gone eastwards (to Bethany and then into the desert) in order to retreat from public life. Or he could have gone westwards (across

the Kidron valley, into the city) and acted as the leader for the many who were all too ready to fight.

Popular acclaim, or peaceful retirement – both would have their attractions for anyone looking to their own interests. Instead Jesus stayed in Gethsemane – this painful, more 'extreme' middle place. Only so could he achieve his own distinctive messianic mission – the royal figure who came to serve, the king who would establish his kingdom not by force but by saving his people from their strongest enemy at great personal cost to himself.

The arrest

At last Judas came, surrounded by a search party of soldiers. It had been a wait of several hours, but when the moment

The Mount of Olives, where Jesus chose to wait. These ancient olive trees near Gethsemane may date back to the 2nd century AD.

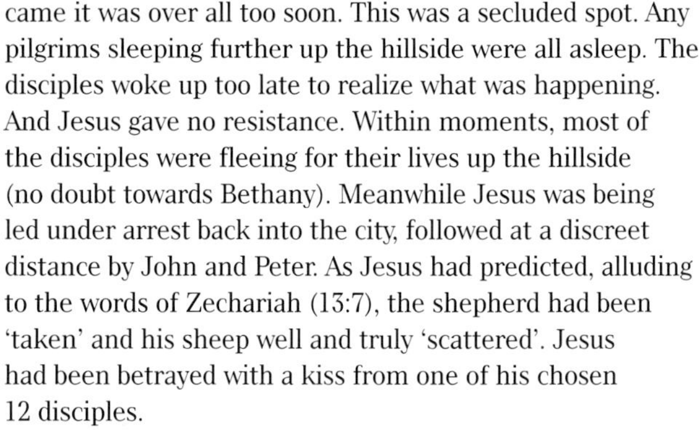

came it was over all too soon. This was a secluded spot. Any pilgrims sleeping further up the hillside were all asleep. The disciples woke up too late to realize what was happening. And Jesus gave no resistance. Within moments, most of the disciples were fleeing for their lives up the hillside (no doubt towards Bethany). Meanwhile Jesus was being led under arrest back into the city, followed at a discreet distance by John and Peter. As Jesus had predicted, alluding to the words of Zechariah (13:7), the shepherd had been 'taken' and his sheep well and truly 'scattered'. Jesus had been betrayed with a kiss from one of his chosen 12 disciples.

He was brought for interrogation first to Annas and then to Annas's son-in-law Caiaphas, who was now the high priest. It was the dead of night, but the high priest's house was a hive of activity – and had been ever since Judas brought his message at around ten o'clock.

Judas betrayed Jesus with a kiss. Scene from the 1964 film *The Gospel According to St Matthew*.

At this point, it becomes important to note that almost certainly the reason Jesus had to wait so long in Gethsemane was not just because the arrest needed to be made when most people were asleep. It was also because some urgent business in the upper city had to be done first. What had been happening in those intervening four or so hours?

The answer is: a lot of discussion and negotiation. The religious authorities had been waiting all week for a suitable moment to arrest Jesus. But Judas's vital piece of information had arrived almost too late – just 20 hours before Passover, which commenced at sundown the next day. If their goal was to remove Jesus, they had very little time in which to secure a conviction and get the all-important clearance from the Roman governor, Pontius Pilate. It is highly probable that Caiaphas decided he must make an urgent late night visit to the governor. Only when they received the green light from him, and could be confident that Jesus really would be executed the next day, was it worth setting out on the expedition to arrest him.

This is conjecture, but it makes sense and explains some otherwise puzzling features in the Gospels: the inclusion of some Roman soldiers in the arresting party (John 18:3); the religious leaders' evident surprise at the trial the next morning when Pilate showed signs of not simply giving the rubber stamp (18:29–30); the oddity of Pilate agreeing to conduct a trial at all on a 'feast day' when the Jewish authorities would not defile themselves by coming inside the Praetorium (18:28); and, last but not least, the strange matter of Pilate's wife (Matthew 27:19). Why did Claudia Procula have a bad dream about Jesus, if it was not that her husband had told her about him the night before?

Interrogation and trial

The prisoner had been arrested and brought in for questioning. Now the task was to secure a conviction. As with other parts of the Gospel accounts, the trial narrative has been bombarded with modern questions. A later Jewish document in the Mishnah suggests it may have been illegal for a defendant to be brought in by soldiers and tried at night. But the accounts themselves bear up well under such interrogation. Yes, perhaps this was strictly illegal, but the urgency of the situation may well have caused such niceties to be overlooked. A proper gathering of the Sanhedrin council could be called as soon as possible after dawn. What was needed now at this preliminary hearing was a confession, or at least some evidence that could be used at a later hearing. A minimum number of two witnesses had to come up with a charge that would stick.

But what would that charge be? They began, as well they might, with that audacious escapade in the temple. Jesus was known to have said something about 'destroying the temple' and raising it 'in three days'. But the witnesses could not agree on the precise wording. In desperation, Caiaphas intervened, placed Jesus under the Oath of the Testimony, and came to the fundamental issue: was Jesus the Messiah? Jesus broke his silence: 'You've said it,' he replied – a Hebraic way of saying 'yes'. 'You will see the Son of man seated at the right hand of the Power and coming with the clouds of heaven' (Mark 14:61–62). Using the colourful prophetic language of Daniel, Jesus was claiming to be the true representative of Israel and the one whom God would manifestly vindicate – yes, even over Caiaphas, the nation's high priest who was about to judge him. This was not quite what Caiaphas was wanting to hear.

But, in another sense, it was. For he could now with confidence present Jesus to the Sanhedrin as a religious

Jewish ossuary box inscribed with the name of Caiaphas, who was high priest at the time of Jesus' trial.

'blasphemer' (because he claimed an exaltation to God's right hand), and to Pilate as a political messianic pretender. Both should be well satisfied.

It had already been a long night, but no one would be sleeping now. The first light of dawn was approaching. The cocks were crowing. Somewhere outside, running through the streets of Jerusalem, there was a man in tears, a former friend of Jesus, who had just denied ever knowing Jesus at all. And he had done so not once, but three times, battered into denial by the simple questions of a servant-girl in the courtyard and the jeers of her friends by the fire. Peter had pledged Jesus unflinching support, but Jesus had known his true colours: 'Before the cock crows twice,' he predicted, 'you will deny me three times' (Mark 14:30). The cock's crowing sounded the death knell to Peter's bravado. The light of dawn broke in on a broken man.

So Jesus was now, even more so, on his own. There would be one or two voices raised in his favour at the dawn Sanhedrin meeting (from members such as Joseph of Arimathea and Nicodemus: John 19:39). But Jesus had done enough to cause the majority to be well convinced that he was a dangerous figure who, for a variety of reasons, needed to be silenced. So he was led before the governor, as arranged, at around eight o'clock in the morning.

The trial before Pilate

But things did not quite go according to plan. Maybe Pilate had done some more thinking during the night and begun to question why he had so readily agreed to fall in with the wishes of the high priest. In the new light of day, he decided instead to be difficult – not out of any respect for this prisoner, whom he had not met, nor for the principles of justice, but as part of his continual battle with the local religious authorities. Why should they get their way? We know from several other events during his 10 years as prefect (AD 26–36) that Pilate had no qualms about causing such offence. He had, for example, brought Roman legions into Jerusalem, and used temple money to finance a new aqueduct. In Luke 13:1, we learn of him killing some Galileans as they were making sacrifices. So he decided not to give the case his rubber stamp. Instead he asked for a formal accusation: 'What charges are you bringing against this man?' (John 18:29).

Maybe there was something about Jesus' manner that suggested this was no ordinary case. Was this silent figure really guilty of something deserving death? He seemed different from the normal revolutionaries with their cursing threats against pagan Rome; if he was claiming to be the Messiah, he was certainly a strange king. So Pilate asked Jesus about his supposed kingdom, and got some unusual answers: 'My kingdom is not of this world… Everyone on the side of truth listens to me.' 'What is truth?' quipped back the cynical governor (John 18:33–38).

'"Where do you come from?" Pilate asked Jesus, but Jesus gave him no answer.'

JOHN 19:9

So Pilate began his evasion tactics. First, he tried sending Jesus round to the residence of Herod Antipas, the tetrarch of Galilee, who was also in town for the feast (Luke 23:6–12). But this was just a delaying tactic: Antipas knew Pilate had the final say and promptly sent the prisoner back. Next he attempted to have Jesus released under the amnesty associated with Passover, whereby one prisoner would be set free for the festival. But the small crowd that was gathering on this otherwise busy day was soon persuaded to ask instead for Barabbas, a murderer who had taken part in an insurrection in Jerusalem (Luke 23:19).

'What shall I do with this Jesus?' Pilate then asked. 'Crucify him,' some shouted, and it soon became a chorus. Around this time Pilate was greeted with further disturbing news – from his wife, who had slept uneasily dreaming about this Jesus: 'Don't have anything to do with that innocent man, for I have suffered a great deal in a dream because of him' (Matthew 27:19). Pilate's present situation, too, was becoming like a bad dream, fast careering out of control.

Pilate had come ready to do battle with the religious authorities. Then, when he first saw the prisoner, he had quickly discovered that he had some good reasons for being awkward. For there was clearly some ulterior motive behind this insistence on Jesus' death, which he suspected included a dose of envy (Matthew 27:18). But, as the accusers were quick to point out, what would the Roman emperor think if Pilate was seen to go 'soft' on someone claiming to be a Messiah or a 'King of the Jews'?

'If you let this man go, you are no friend of Caesar.'

JOHN 19:12

So, eventually, the death sentence was issued. But Pilate made it clear it was not in accord with his own wishes. He took a bowl of water and washed his hands (Matthew 27:24). It was meant to be a symbol of Pilate's innocence, but you could equally see it as a complete abrogation of responsibility.

The sins of human history

As with the 'trial' before Caiaphas, this Roman trial has naturally been subjected to endless scrutiny. Most importantly, have the evangelists been unduly influenced by their intention to portray Jesus' innocence or even their desire to place the responsibility onto the Jewish authorities? These are questions made more sensitive by the way this episode has subsequently been abused as an excuse for anti-Jewish sentiment.

None of that later abuse of history can be excused. For the Gospels are clear that, at a deeper level, all of us have contributed to this event; Jesus was 'rejected by humankind' as a whole (1 Peter 2:4). The rejection he experienced on that one occasion is symptomatic of the rejection he experiences from us all. Nor can people be held to account for the actions of their distant forbears.

On the other hand, the truths of history cannot be rewritten so as to prevent such abuse. For the historian has to explain an unpleasant fact of history: namely that Jesus, despite the strong evidence that he was not stirring revolt against Rome, was crucified on a Roman cross.

The Gospels give us an adequate explanation – one

Facing page: The huge platform supporting the temple dominated Jerusalem. Across the Kidron valley from the temple was the Mount of Olives, with the Garden of Gethsemane on its lower slopes. The traditional site of Jesus' crucifixion is to the west of the city, but the likely route to that site is disputed.

that does credit neither to the Roman authorities, nor to the Jewish authorities, nor to the disciples themselves. It is a sorry indictment of everyone, except Jesus. But it rings true to life – a window into the self-interests of the human heart. When we ask why Jesus was crucified, there is no one simple explanation as the causes are so multi-layered. But we do see the full range of human sin: the greed of Judas, the ignorance and timidity of the disciples, the envy and political agendas of the Jewish authorities, the cowardice and naked self-interest of the Roman governor. It is an indictment of us all.

The way to the cross

So Jesus was flogged and led out from the Praetorium to be crucified. To begin with he carried his own cross beam (or patibulum), but when he collapsed the soldiers requisitioned the help of a man coming into the city at that moment, Simon of Cyrene. The small party would have passed through the 'Gennath' (or 'Garden') gate

Where was Jesus crucified?

'The Place of the Skull' near the 'Garden tomb'.

Jesus was crucified at a 'place called Golgotha (which means The Place of the Skull)' (Mark 15:22) and buried in a nearby tomb (John 19:41). Crucifixions in Jerusalem were not that common, but this may have been the place regularly used for any executions – hence the macabre name. Alternatively, some features may have resembled a skull in some way. Despite later tradition, the Bible nowhere talks of it as a hill.

The exact location is still disputed. Because of ritual defilement and uncleanness, no tombs were ever inside a city's wall. The 'Garden tomb' site was certainly outside the wall, but is the same true for the traditional site, now marked by the Church of the Holy Sepulchre? The early church traditions are more cogent than some think, but final certainty may elude us.

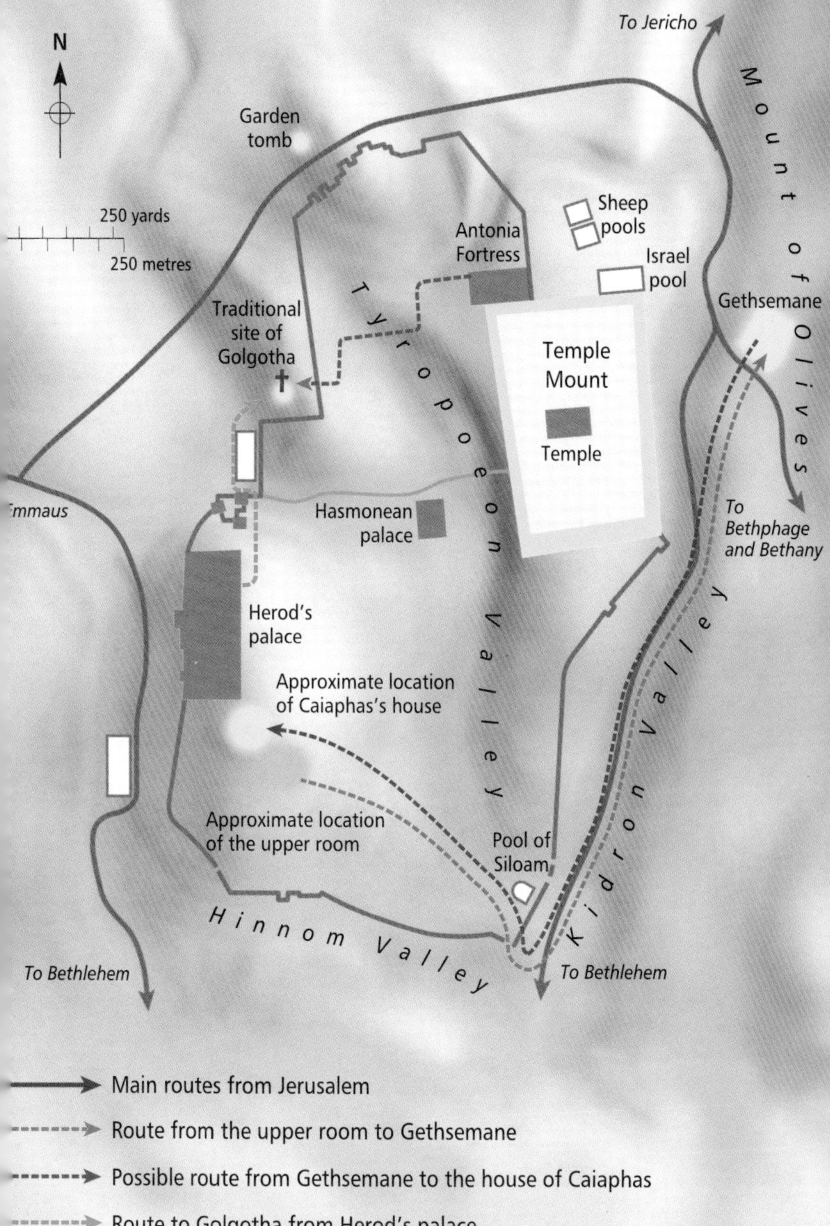
N
To Jericho
Mount of Olives
Garden tomb
250 yards
250 metres
Sheep pools
Antonia Fortress
Israel pool
Gethsemane
Traditional site of Golgotha
Tyropoeon Valley
Temple Mount
Temple
Emmaus
Hasmonean palace
To Bethphage and Bethany
Herod's palace
Kidron Valley
Approximate location of Caiaphas's house
Approximate location of the upper room
Pool of Siloam
Hinnom Valley
To Bethlehem
To Bethlehem
Main routes from Jerusalem
Route from the upper room to Gethsemane
Possible route from Gethsemane to the house of Caiaphas
Route to Golgotha from Herod's palace
Alternative route to Golgotha from Antonia Fortress (along Via Dolorosa)

towards a place outside the city walls appropriately called 'Golgotha' ('Place of the Skull'). And 'there they crucified him', between two brigands.

The Gospels are remarkably restrained in their description. Their account is bald and unemotional. They pass over the shameful fact that Jesus almost certainly hung naked on the cross, but they hint at it by talking of the soldiers casting lots for his clothing. They do not comment on how people were feeling, nor exactly who was there. Of Jesus' male disciples, the only one we can be sure was present was John – though Peter, despite his grief, may have been unable to stay away. They mention instead

Jesus was crucified between two 'bandits'. Scene from the 1979 film *Jesus*.

some women, who included Mary Magdalene and (for a while) Jesus' own mother.

The Gospel writers also describe some of the comments of those watching. There is a powerful interchange between Jesus and one of those crucified with him, and also a prayer: 'Father, forgive them, for they do not know what they are doing' (Luke 23:34). But, for the most part, the Gospel accounts are brief and to the point.

Even when viewed just 'on the surface' and within its own historical setting it remains a powerful scene. For the

The life of Jesus: his crucifixion

Crucifixion was recognized as the most barbaric form of death, reserved for slaves and political rebels. For the Jews, it seemed even worse: the victim was normally left to hang naked, and their scriptures suggested that anyone hanging 'on a tree' was under God's curse (Deuteronomy 21:23). The nails were probably hammered through the victim's forearms and then, because of the body's weight, they would tear through the flesh until they reached the wrist. Victims eventually died of suffocation, unable to pull themselves up sufficiently to breathe.

Jesus died more quickly than some, but not before he had said some memorable words, which speak of forgiveness, of spiritual agony, but also of triumphant purpose: 'Father, forgive them, for they know not what they do'; 'My God, my God, why have you forsaken me?'; and, at the end, 'It is completed!'

Christians ever since have seen this not just as a human story but as the act of God himself, giving himself to save his people: 'God demonstrates his own love in this: while we were yet sinners, Christ died for us' (Romans 6:8).

Roman soldiers, it was just another day of routine business, but the centurion seems to have sensed something strange going on: 'Surely he was the Son of God!' he declared (Matthew 27:54). There were many in the crowds who had seen such things before and whose chief worry was more about being ready for the feast that night; but there was an eerie darkness over the city. And soon there was talk of an unusual event in the temple: the curtain in front of the Holy of Holies, which symbolized the separation of sinful people from the holy presence of God, had suddenly been ripped in two (Mark 14:33, 38). Was this a new way into God's presence being opened up? At the very least, something dramatic was happening.

'You who are going to destroy the temple and build it in three days, come down from the cross and save yourself!'

MARK 15:29–30

The unwanted king

In the midst of all this, there was a man upon a cross whom most knew should not be there. Despite what his accusers had said to Pilate (Luke 23:2) he was not 'opposed to paying taxes' to Rome; nor was he an instigator of violent revolt. However, his accusers were correct in some of their charges. There was a sense in which he was 'subverting the nation'. He was laying a challenge to the Israel of his day and, if he had been right, then the people should have responded and come round to his cause.

Moreover it was quite true that he had 'claimed to be the Messiah, the king'. Pilate ordered this charge to be placarded on the cross in three languages: 'Jesus of Nazareth: King of the Jews'. Yet, though such royal claims were no doubt dangerous in the eyes of Rome, it was hardly a crime in itself; after all, people supposedly longed for the Messiah to come. The problem was that the Messiah was not expected to have this kind of radical agenda. He was supposed to pronounce blessing on 'us' and judgment on 'them'. This kind of Messiahship, this upside-down kind of kingdom, must be declared false, and its proponent prevented from leading others astray.

And so, at around three o'clock in the afternoon just

outside the wall of the capital city, there died a man whose crime, as expressed on the wooden plaque above his head, was simply that of being 'the King of the Jews'. Was he?

His friends and opponents went back to their homes. Not unnaturally, they thought it was all over.

CHAPTER 11

The Following Sunday

Death is normally the end: the crucifixion should have been the end of the story. The disciples' hopes should have died with Jesus. The plight of Israel was unchanged, the Romans had not gone away. Instead the Romans had snuffed out this messianic claimant with their brutal method of execution reserved for slaves and criminals. No doubt Jesus had left an impressive example and also said some marvellous things about God, some of which might be salvaged and passed on to others. But now that Jesus' fate had been sealed, and his God revealed as no more able to save than any other, this Jesus of Nazareth was really not worth bothering about. His ministry had been a 'nine-day wonder', a brief ray of light in an otherwise depressingly black sky.

The after-effects of a dead Messiah

It is worth looking seriously at this issue. Too often, in both the scholarly and popular worlds, people think you can leave Jesus dead and still explain why he has been followed by millions of people ever since. But when you stop for a moment to think historically, and to imagine what the crucifixion would have meant on its own terms, you very soon realize that this is most unlikely. A dead Messiah is a failed Messiah. There's simply no point in trying to rescue or raise anything out of that mess.

For at some point, the historian is going to have to explain what evidently happened in the years following Jesus' death: the surprising proclamation of Jesus as the successful Messiah; the announcement that the kingdom of God had truly been established; the transformation of the timid disciples into fearless spokesmen for his cause; the rapid spread of the message about Jesus outside the boundaries of Judaism; and the fact that to this day Jesus is still the most talked-about figure from ancient history – with nearly a third of the current world's population claiming to be among his followers.

Something somewhere must explain this otherwise quite disproportionate result. After all, crucified criminals do not normally have this kind of effect. As an analogy, if we see a rocket flying through space, we are justified in presuming that it only got there because first it was launched: no launch, no rocket in sky. In the same way, when we look at the subsequent phenomenon of how Jesus has been followed, we are entitled to ask what launched it. Can we find anything sufficient to explain this extraordinary result?

'If Jesus is not raised, redemptive history ends in the cul-de-sac of a Palestinian grave.'

G.E. LADD, *THE RESURRECTION OF CHRIST*, 1975

The New Testament writers offer us an explanation: Jesus did not stay dead but was raised by God to new life 'on the third day'. This may sound extraordinary, but if that is indeed what happened, then all those after-effects begin to make sense. A risen Messiah is quite different from a crucified one.

The resurrection: the evidence of history

Resurrection is not, of course, the kind of thing you normally find discussed in historical biographies of great figures from the past. We are clearly moving into new and unfamiliar ground at this point. In fact, some would claim that when we start talking of the resurrection we have entirely left the field of proper 'history' and have entered instead into some vague world of faith and spirituality. Often this means, for example, that the 'historical Jesus' is deemed to mean only the 'pre-Easter' Jesus. Anything that may or may not have happened after his crucifixion is ruled out of court as non-historical.

But proper history does not select in advance what it

will choose to uncover; nor does it decide what is allowed to have taken place. It responds to the evidence and tries to offer a hypothesis that will best explain the events. When looked at in this way, some have come to quite the reverse conclusion: that the resurrection of Jesus is one of the best-attested facts of ancient history. If so, then a book such as this about Jesus' historical life cannot suddenly stop at the moment of his crucifixion. It must look at the possibility of Jesus' historical existence after his death.

What, then, is the evidence for Jesus' return to life? The two earliest accounts of what happened come from

Two Easter passages

For what I received I passed on to you as of first importance: that Christ died for our sins according to the scriptures, that he was buried, that he was raised on the third day according to the scriptures, and that he appeared to Peter, and then to the Twelve. After that, he appeared to more than five hundred of the brothers at the same time, most of whom are still living…

1 CORINTHIANS 15:3–6

When the Sabbath was over, Mary Magdalene, Mary the mother of James, and Salome bought spices so that they might go to anoint Jesus' body. Very early on the first day of the week, just after sunrise, they were on their way to the tomb and they asked each other, 'Who will roll the stone away from the entrance of the tomb?' But when they looked up, they saw that the stone, which was very large, had been rolled away. As they entered the tomb, they saw a young man dressed in a white robe sitting on the right side, and they were alarmed.

'Don't be alarmed,' he said. 'You are looking for Jesus the Nazarene, who was crucified. He has risen! He is not here. See the place where they laid him.'… Trembling and bewildered, the women went out and fled from the tomb. They said nothing to anyone because they were afraid.

MARK 16:1–6, 8

Paul's first letter to the church in Corinth (written c. AD 55) and Mark's Gospel (probably written c. AD 67) (see 'Two Easter passages', page 157). Needless to say, thousands of words have been written about these and the many other New Testament passages that speak of Jesus' resurrection. After all, the stakes are very high. If these early witnesses are right, something unparalleled in the rest of human history took place outside Jerusalem's walls on that first Easter Sunday morning.

The early evidence

Several features within these texts suggest that it did. Note first the early nature of this evidence. Paul is writing within 25 years of the event, and lays down the challenge that many of those who saw the risen Jesus were still alive to testify to the fact. This extraordinary claim was not being made about some long-distant historical person, but instead about someone who had walked the streets of Jerusalem within living memory.

Moreover, Paul's words may reflect a well-worn formula. He is reminding the Corinthians of the teaching which he had taught them some years earlier and which he himself had received from others – no doubt the first disciples of Jesus whom Paul met in Jerusalem a few years after his conversion. Paul is asserting that this resurrection claim goes back to the earliest days of the church's existence. If he is using a set formula, that would suggest this was a standard part of Christian teaching – used repeatedly.

'Christianity stands or falls with the reality of the raising of Jesus from the dead by God.'

JURGEN MOLTMANN, *THEOLOGY OF HOPE*, 1967

So the resurrection claim was an early and foundational part of Christianity. According to Acts 2 it was the central theme of Jesus' first followers as they spoke in Jerusalem within weeks of the event.

Meanwhile, although Mark's account may only have been published in written form after Paul's time, it has all the hallmarks of a fresh remembering of an unforgettable event. It is not a well-polished 'set piece' but contains all the rough edges one might expect in an account of a

sudden and unexpected occurrence. In fact, a story outline similar to Mark's could well have been part of the 'oral tradition' that Paul then received when he made that visit to Jerusalem in the mid-30s.

Some have tried to suggest that this is impossible; they argue that the fact that Paul does not explicitly mention the 'tomb' in his account means he may not have known about the 'empty tomb' traditions. But his clear reference to Jesus' 'burial' implies his awareness of the tomb and his belief that the Jesus who was physically dead was also physically resurrected. Paul would have had no problems at all with Mark's account. Both Mark and Paul, despite their different interests (the one telling the 'empty tomb' story, the other summarizing the appearances), are recounting very early traditions.

When Mary Magdalene, Mary, the mother of James, and Salome came to anoint Jesus' body after the Sabbath, they found that the stone had been rolled away from the entrance of the tomb.

The unexpected event

Secondly, there is the element of surprise. Paul and Mark make plain that Jesus' resurrection was not something that they themselves were expecting. Paul himself was originally no friend of this early Christian message but one of its fiercest opponents. He thought all this talk of the crucified Messiah was sheer madness, if not outright blasphemy. But then he had an encounter with the risen Jesus on the road to Damascus (Acts 9). This was such a shock to his system that he had to go into the desert for three years to think through his whole belief-system from scratch.

Likewise the women venturing towards the tomb were caught totally by surprise. They went to pay their final respects to Jesus and to finish off properly the task of his burial. But when they got there, their plans were aborted. There was no body; the place where he had been lying was deserted. Even if, with hindsight, the disciples could look back on some occasions when Jesus had hinted at his resurrection, they clearly had not understood what he was talking about (see, for example, Mark 9:10). This event took them all completely by surprise.

It was not, then, something they were looking for; nor did they invent it to make themselves feel good. On the contrary, it was a dramatic event that for all its positive repercussions was initially bewildering and unsettling. They were not comforting themselves with a fiction; they were confronted by a fact.

The variety of resurrection appearances

Thirdly, it is worth noting who exactly it was that supposedly encountered the risen Jesus, and also when and where they did so. The four Gospel accounts are remarkable in asserting that the first people to discover the empty tomb were women. Given that in those days a woman's evidence was not admissible in a court of law, there is no way that anyone would ever have invented such a story. It lays the whole claim open to ridicule – hardly the kind of thing that Jesus' male disciples would have concocted.

Paul's account is interesting, too. Yes, he concentrates on Jesus' appearances to the apostles, but he clearly speaks about some occasions when Jesus was seen not just by individuals but by whole groups – 'all the apostles' or a

Burial practices at the time of Jesus

As the Sabbath was approaching, Jesus' body was only temporarily laid to rest – not necessarily in the final location that his followers intended. He was laid just inside the tomb and the rolling stone placed across the entrance – not least to keep out scavenging animals. Other examples of 1st-century rolling stones give us an idea of their size (around 75 cm in diameter) and how they slotted into position. In normal circumstances, a body would decompose within a year, then the bones would be removed from the burial shelf and placed in an ossuary box.

group of 500. This reminds us that, according to Acts, there was a period of some '40 days' during which Jesus gave 'many convincing proofs that he was alive' (Acts 1:3). So these appearances did not occur only on that first Sunday, nor indeed only in Jerusalem (see, for example, Luke 24:13, Matthew 28:16 and John 21:1). Instead they took place over a reasonably extended period, giving people sufficient time to begin to process the implications. This encounter with the reality of Jesus' resurrection was not something that was all over in an instant, nor was it all done 'in a corner' (Acts 26:26). There was time and opportunity for its reality to be questioned and verified.

So there are some initial signs that we should take this claim very seriously indeed. Nevertheless, there are a string of other objections that inevitably come up at this point, which we also need to consider briefly.

Divergent accounts?

For a start, the different accounts of the resurrection are sometimes thought to be slightly conflicting, or even in total contradiction. To be sure, when we add to the above two accounts (from Mark and 1 Corinthians) the other

This tomb with its rolling stone gives us an idea of how the tomb in which Jesus' body was placed may have looked.

three main accounts (in Matthew, John and Luke–Acts), the picture that emerges is not completely straightforward; they may be drawing on some different sources for their material. So, for example, Luke has no resurrection appearances in Galilee. Meanwhile only Matthew speaks of an earthquake at the time of Jesus' resurrection and of the guards being placed at the tomb by the chief priests. There is some confusion, too, concerning the 'young man' (Mark 16:5) who spoke to the women in the tomb. Matthew speaks instead of an 'angel', Luke of 'two men in clothes that gleamed like lightning' (Matthew 28:5; Luke 24:4).

Many have responded to these criticisms by saying that a few such differences do not mean the whole story is itself an invention. No one doubts that Hannibal crossed the Alps just because we cannot fully reconstruct his route. Or again, for a more recent example, there were clear discrepancies of detail in some of the first newspaper reports describing the attack on the World Trade Center, but no one could use this to doubt the reality of that tragedy. Once we recognize this, we begin to sense it would only be if this resurrection story were a complete fabrication that we might expect to have a watertight version – fully agreed upon by the inventors prior to circulation. So the existence of these variants in detail suggests instead that the main thrust of the accounts is probably reliable.

Others argue that the different accounts can indeed be reconciled with one another. Once you allow for some of the authors' different interests and perspectives, their selection of different material makes perfect sense. Later we will lay out just one of the possible ways in which the period of Jesus' resurrection appearances can be summarized. It is a powerful story and it hangs together remarkably well even after all these years.

The various accounts do stand up to close scrutiny. Taken together they suggest that we are dealing here with a true story, vividly remembered. Of course the writers are fully aware that this is also a very odd story – they had never experienced anything like this before – but they try to impress upon us that this was in fact what happened.

Ultimately, however, irrespective of our view of the exact reliability of the various accounts, there are only two options for what actually happened 'on the ground'. Either the tomb was empty or it was not. Those who question the reality of Jesus' physical resurrection cannot have it both ways. And it is then entirely legitimate to push such questioners further down their chosen line of reasoning to see whether their objections to the resurrection really make sense.

So let's now look briefly in turn at these two different lines of enquiry. Can an explanation other than the traditional one be reasonably built up from them?

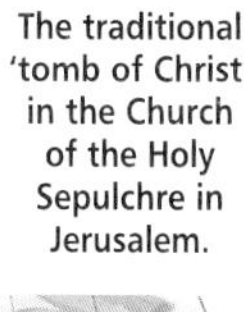

The traditional 'tomb of Christ' in the Church of the Holy Sepulchre in Jerusalem.

Option 1: the tomb was empty

Those in the first camp acknowledge the overwhelming likelihood that Jesus' tomb was indeed empty. They realize how odd it would have looked for anyone in Jerusalem to claim that Jesus was raised from the dead when his corpse was still in the tomb. No, they agree, the tomb must have been empty. For such people, the oldest explanation ever offered (that the disciples had stolen the body: Matthew 28:13) is itself strong evidence that the tomb was recognized by all to be empty. What they have to do is to offer an explanation for it being empty.

Perhaps Jesus' body was indeed stolen? Or perhaps he never truly died and so walked out of the tomb after a three-day period of recuperation? This latter idea, sometimes called the 'swoon theory', only came into fashion in the 18th century. But did the Roman soldiers really fail to kill their prisoner? Most unlikely. Moreover John recounts that when Jesus' body was pierced on the cross, blood and water came out separately (19:34). This phenomenon, now known to modern medicine, was a sign that death had already taken place. And if by some miracle Jesus had indeed survived this ordeal, is it really likely that he would feel so much better after lying unattended for 36 hours with open and bleeding wounds on a cold damp slab? Would he really have been able to push up that entrenched rolling stone and convince people that he was to be worshipped as the Lord of life? On the contrary, he would surely have been in need of urgent medical attention.

As for Jesus' body being stolen, the question is: who would have wanted to do this? The Jewish authorities would have done anything to produce the body, not steal it. So, too, the Romans. And what would have made them do it in the first place?

Others have suggested it was the disciples who stole the body. But everything suggests that they were in no mood for this risky kind of game. Most were in hiding throughout the weekend and, when they did pluck up courage to meet in Jerusalem, it was behind locked doors (John 20:19). To remove Jesus' corpse would have been a capital offence and attracted attention. This was not exactly what they wanted. Given the circumstances, they had done well to secure for Jesus such a decent burial. So when the women first found the tomb disturbed, their immediate fear was precisely that someone else must have stolen their master's corpse.

Just supposing the disciples had played out this charade, how did they live out this hoax for the rest of their lives? Many of the disciples would die because of what they claimed about Jesus and his resurrection. Why didn't any of them give way under pressure? Their subsequent behaviour suggests instead that they were thoroughly convinced the tomb was empty.

So if the tomb was empty, how do we explain it? Yes, Jesus had been truly dead and buried, but who would have wanted to steal his body, or been able to? This line of enquiry only forces us to consider again the possibility that Jesus really was raised from the dead.

Option 2: Jesus' body was still in the tomb

Some have argued that the body was in the tomb all along. The women may have gone to the wrong tomb. Others argue that there was in fact no contradiction in the disciples' proclamation of Jesus' resurrection while his body was still in the tomb: they were talking about a purely 'spiritual' experience.

With regard to the first point, little needs to be said. It wouldn't have taken much for someone to point out to the women their mistake. The second argument, however, needs a more careful response – not least because it is quite common in some circles today.

It is a far from convincing argument, however. Most significantly, the very word 'resurrection' speaks out against it. In Greek, the word for 'resurrection' (*anastasis*) has the literal meaning of 'making to stand up'. By the time of Jesus it had already become the standard word to express what Jews believed God would do for his faithful people at the end of time. God would raise people physically from their graves, making them 'stand up', at the end of time. This was a common belief, for example, among the Pharisees (see, for example, Acts 23:6–9). What was so odd about the first Christians was not so much their talk about 'resurrection' but their conviction that God had now done this for one unique individual in the middle of human history.

The important point to note is this: the apostles were not talking about something purely 'spiritual'. Nor would they have been heard in such terms by their contemporaries. This was not a pious wish that Jesus' 'spirit' should go 'marching on'. Nor were they talking about a 'resurrection' of their own faith in Jesus. This was

'That a few simple men should in one generation have invented so powerful and appealing a personality, so lofty an ethic and so inspiring a vision of human brotherhood, would be a miracle far more incredible than any recorded in the Gospels.'

WILL DURANT, *CAESAR AND CHRIST*, 1947

The life of Jesus: his resurrection appearances

Saturday (the day after the crucifixion)

Mary Magdalene and another Mary (the mother of James) buy spices when the Sabbath ends at sunset and walk to Bethany with Cleopas to be reunited with nine of Jesus' male disciples (last seen fleeing from Gethsemane in the early hours of Friday morning).

The chief priests ask Pilate for a guard to be set on the tomb.

Sunday (the 'third day')

The resurrection of Jesus (perhaps coinciding with an earthquake).

The two Marys and Cleopas set out at cockcrow for John's house in the upper city, where they meet up with another woman called Salome. She joins the two Marys and they go to the tomb. When they see the tomb entrance disturbed, Mary Magdalene (the youngest) runs back to John's house to alert Peter and John.

Joanna and Susanna arrive from the Hasmonean palace, where they are in the retinue of Herod Antipas; the four women now go into the tomb. When they see the strange figure in the tomb and hear him speaking to them, they flee in panic. Meanwhile, Peter and John arrive at the tomb and go in.

Later, Mary Magdalene returns to the tomb on her own, much distressed, and is the first to meet the risen Jesus. Two of the women meet Jesus, perhaps en route to the disciples in Bethany. Hearing the news, the disciples at last pluck up courage to return to the city. At some point, Jesus meets Simon Peter (somewhere on his own – perhaps in Gethsemane?).

Cleopas and his companion meet Jesus on their walk to Emmaus; they return immediately to Jerusalem and to the upper room in Mark's house, arriving in the evening. Once there, the risen Jesus appears 'to all the disciples except Thomas'.

The next five weeks

One week later, Jesus appears to the disciples again in the upper room, this time with Thomas present. At some point, he also meets with his previously cynical younger brother, James. The disciples return briefly to Galilee and meet Jesus both by the lakeside and on a mountain. The meeting of 500 with Jesus takes place in this period.

The disciples return to Jerusalem after three weeks or so and have their last meeting with the risen Jesus on the Mount of Olives, not far from Bethany. Jesus' ascension then brings this unique period of resurrection appearances to a close.

'Then their eyes were opened and they recognized him.' *Christ in Emmaus* by Michelangelo Merisi da Caravaggio (1573–1610).

a claim about something that had happened not to them, but to Jesus. Christ was raised, not just in the faith of his followers, but in reality and within his own life story. The resurrection only became a series of experiences for believers because it was first an event for Jesus.

So when they spoke about Jesus' 'resurrection', they would have been heard to be making a claim for the physical body of Jesus – that it was no longer visibly dead. If so, the corpse cannot have been still in the tomb. That would have contradicted their claim immediately. No, the tomb was empty. Everyone at the time seems to have agreed about that. The point at issue was: where was Jesus now?

The disciples had their answer: God had raised him to new life. And they were convinced of this for the simple reason that the risen Jesus had appeared to them on several occasions. An empty tomb on its own might be explained away in other ways. It is these resurrection appearances, when backed up by the traditions of the empty tomb, which then form the basis for this extraordinary claim – Jesus had come back from the dead.

The resurrection of Jesus

'Without the resurrection, the New Testament loses its soul and Christian faith its central pillar.'

MURRAY HARRIS, *RAISED IMMORTAL*, 1983

Whichever way you look at it, then, there are remarkably good historical grounds for accepting the apostles' claim for the physical resurrection of Jesus' body. This explanation makes more sense than other supposedly 'historical' reconstructions.

It also makes sense of the otherwise puzzling resurrection appearances of Jesus. For all their oddity, these can now be seen as genuine encounters with a person who had been through death and had come out the other side – a person who had a 'spiritual body' (that is, a physical body fully animated by God's Spirit). These appearances do not have to be interpreted as some kind of mass hallucination. This was always a most unlikely explanation; but given what modern research has revealed about hallucinations it is now even less likely.

The resurrection means that we will only properly understand Jesus when we view his life from the vantage point of its surprising climax. If Jesus was not raised from the dead, then what we have studied so far has only a limited value. He taught great things, but we do not have any evidence that the God of whom he spoke actually exists. Yes, he was a brilliant human being, but that only makes the rest of us feel rather awkward in comparison. He gave up his life for his own cause, but we are not too sure what that cause was exactly, or what, if anything, it was intended to achieve. So we are left with a dynamic figure who entered the turbulent world of 1st-century Palestine and shone there for a brief moment, only to disappear.

If, on the other hand, Jesus really was raised from the dead by God, his whole life comes to be seen in a new light. His teaching now comes with the evident backing and authority of the God of Israel. His character gives us insight, not just into humanity, but into the very heart of God himself. And his death begins to be seen not as a waste but as a wonder – the love of God at work to heal and rescue his broken world. Moreover, if Jesus was raised, the historical Jesus is not just a figure of the past, nor indeed is history the only way of discovering him. He is alive today. He may have the capacity to walk out of the history books and into the present.

So we, too, cannot leave the matter at this point and 'close the book' on Jesus. For we seem to be dealing here with someone who refused to be left dead and buried in his allotted grave. And he still asks those awkward, but kind, questions: 'Who do you say that I am?' and 'What do you want me to do for you?' (Mark 8:29; 10:51).

CHAPTER 12

Jesus' Followers Reflect

Previous pages: The risen Jesus appeared to his disciples on at least two occasions in their home area around Lake Galilee.

In this final chapter, we examine what Jesus' first followers came to say about him. What was it that had disturbed the peace in the land of Palestine? Just who exactly was Jesus? Whole libraries have been written on this one issue. All we can do here is make a few introductory comments. So we will trace through the early pages of Luke's account of the early church (called the Acts of the Apostles; see 'Extracts from Peter's sermons', page 173), noting some of the very first things said about Jesus, and then draw in other voices from elsewhere in the New Testament.

Primitive but powerful

Of course, there are some who think that speeches such as Peter's in Acts are complete fabrications. No doubt there has been some editing by Luke. Yet it is remarkable how much they seem to reflect the thoughts of Jesus' very first followers. For example, the descriptions of Jesus as the 'servant' or as the 'prophet' foretold by Moses are not developed much by other New Testament writers – precisely because they wanted to say that Jesus was so much more. So when these titles are used here of Jesus, Luke is quite probably recapturing the feel of those first explosive days in Jerusalem. He might well have had eyewitnesses or written sources to help him.

These speeches have an authentic ring to them. Scholars may label them 'primitive' when compared with the rest of the New Testament, but that does not

Extracts from Peter's sermons

Jesus of Nazareth was a man accredited by God to you by miracles, wonders and signs… He was handed over to you by God's set purpose… But God raised him from the dead… because it was impossible for death to keep its hold on him… David knew that God had promised him… that he would place one of his descendants on his throne… Therefore let all Israel be assured of this: God has made this Jesus, whom you crucified, both Lord and Christ.

ACTS 2:22, 23, 24, 30, 36

The God of Abraham, Isaac and Jacob, the God of our fathers, has glorified his servant Jesus… You disowned the Holy and Righteous One… You killed the author of life, but God raised him from the dead… Repent… that God may send the Christ, who has been appointed for you – even Jesus… For Moses said, 'The Lord your God will raise up for you a prophet like me… You must listen to everything he tells you' [Deuteronomy 18:15]… God said to Abraham, 'Through your offspring all peoples on earth will be blessed' [Genesis 22:18]. When God raised up his servant, he sent him first to you to bless you.

ACTS 3:13, 14, 15, 19, 20, 22, 25–26

He is 'the stone you builders rejected, which has become the capstone' [Psalm 118:22]. Salvation is found in no one else, for there is no other name… by which we must be saved… God exalted him to his own right hand as Prince and Saviour that he might give… forgiveness of sins to Israel.

ACTS 4:11–12; 5:31

God commanded us… to testify that he is the one whom God appointed as judge of the living and the dead. All the prophets testify about him that everyone who believes in him receives forgiveness of sins through his name.

ACTS 10:42–43

Peter clearly was convinced about the resurrection of Jesus. It was the indispensable basis of his message. Time and again, he asserts that God 'raised him from the dead' and has now 'exalted him to his right hand' in heaven. Put simply – no resurrection, no message.

stop them from being profound. They certainly contain within them all the powerful seeds that would later come to maturity elsewhere. What are the implications, for example, of the seemingly casual remark that Jesus had been the 'author of life'? Within a Jewish context, where the only creator of life was the God of Israel, such a phrase was indeed like dynamite. But Peter, rejoicing in the recent resurrection, lets it all come out. His words are pristine but powerful as he begins to express what no one before had ever needed to express. He makes four key claims for the person of Jesus.

Claim 1: Jesus, the fulfilment of Israel's hope

Note, first, Peter's conviction that Jesus can only be understood when set in his Jewish context. There is no idea that Jesus is starting a new religion. The gospel story is a story of the activity of the God of Israel. It is a story of how God's promises to Israel and to the world have now been fulfilled in Jesus. Ever since King David, Israel had been longing for a new king like David to sit on his throne; now, says Peter, we have been given one by God – his name is Jesus and his throne is an everlasting one, not in Jerusalem but at the Father's right hand. Ever since Moses, Israel has been looking for a 'prophet like Moses': now we have one. Since the time of Abraham, the divine promise has been to bless the nations through his descendants: now through Jesus (Abraham's offspring par excellence) that blessing is at last coming to pass – first for Israel, then for the world.

In all these ways, the Jesus-story is plugged immediately and directly into the much longer story of Israel. Indeed, it is portrayed as its crowning moment. Straightaway we note that there is no true description of Jesus that does not connect him in a vital way to the God of Israel. Peter is announcing to Israel the fulfilment of her covenant, the great climactic moment to which all of Israel's extended history has been straining. This is the moment they had been waiting for.

This then explains the way the apostles immediately start to plunder the Old Testament for passages that can help to explain the import of Jesus. Just in these few excerpts (see 'Extracts from Peter's sermons', page 173), you can see Peter quoting Genesis, Deuteronomy and several Psalms, as well as alluding to passages in 2 Samuel and Isaiah.

Subsequent 'Christian' interpretations of Jesus have sometimes played down his Jewishness. Indeed, someone called Marcion (around AD 150) went so far as to teach that the Old Testament was some kind of mistake – the work of a 'lesser god' compared with the God revealed in Jesus. Such thinking is dangerous, wrenching Jesus from his context. To understand Jesus we must never forget that he was thoroughly Jewish. What makes him distinct, however, even within that Jewish context, is the claim that he is the unique fulfilment of Jewish hope. If there has been a 'parting of the ways' between Judaism and Christianity, it is not because Jesus was somehow pro-Gentile or even anti-Jewish. If anything, it is quite the reverse. He was so Jewish and so central to Jewish life as to be heralded by his followers as the true fulfilment and indeed the very embodiment of Israel's destiny and hope. This is the point that causes the controversy.

Claim 2: Jesus the Messiah, the rejected king

The chief title used of Jesus in these passages is Messiah (or, in Greek, the 'Christ'); the term implies that Jesus embodies in his own person the destiny of Israel. 'Christ' is sometimes treated as if it were Jesus' surname – just another, interchangeable name. But that is to rob it of its original, powerful meaning. Throughout most of the New Testament it retains its function as a title; it is a claim for Jesus as the long-awaited Messiah of Israel. What thrills Peter about the resurrection is that it has shown Jesus to be Israel's true Messiah: 'God has made this Jesus to be Lord and Christ'; Jesus is the 'Christ' who has been 'appointed for you'.

Various hopes were attached to the idea of the Messiah – not least that he would rid Israel of pagan domination. But now, despite the fact that outwardly Israel's national and political life remained unchanged, Peter was claiming that the Messiah had indeed come. What made him do it? The only possible answer is the resurrection. No resurrection, no messianic claim.

Few people would doubt that the first followers of Jesus proclaimed him as Messiah; the very nickname

In Greek, the initial letters of 'Jesus Christ, Son of God, Saviour' spell 'ICHTHUS' – the word for 'fish'. Early Christian inscription from the catacomb of Domitilla, Rome.

they earned – as the 'Christians' or 'messianics' – speaks volumes as to what they were constantly talking about. What people often fail to realize, however, is that this solid evidence (that Christians resolutely proclaimed Jesus as the 'Christ') is itself strong evidence for his physical resurrection. Given the additional expectations that people had for the Messiah (some of which Jesus had not fulfilled – at least apparently), Christians could only have launched this campaign for Jesus as Messiah if they were forced to it by something as unexpected and as unlikely as a resurrection. After all, if Jesus had remained physically dead, none of them would have dared to promote him as Messiah. The whole idea was a complete non-starter – not least because this Messiah, far from defeating the Romans, had ended up being crucified by them.

So, the Christians' claim for Jesus as Messiah only makes sense if they were convinced of his physical resurrection. This was God's way of vindicating his true servant, or – if you like – of redefining the 'job description' of the Messiah.

So, according to Peter and Jesus' followers, Jesus is God's chosen king. Although he had not been born in a palace and had been rejected by his own people, he was God's 'anointed prince'. Jesus had humbly proclaimed the kingdom of God, but now through his resurrection he was revealed as the king of that kingdom! God was reigning through Jesus.

Claim 3: Jesus the Lord

There was, however, an even more startling claim: 'God has made this Jesus both *Lord* and Christ' (Acts 2:36). In certain contexts, this word 'Lord' (*kurios* in Greek) need only mean the equivalent of a 'boss'. At other times, however, it includes notions of total power and authority – for example, when the Roman emperors wanted their subjects to confess that Caesar was 'Lord'. Most important of all, in a Jewish context it could also speak of God himself – as it does frequently in the Greek translation of the Old Testament, the Septuagint.

'He is the image of the invisible God... by whom all things were created... God was pleased to have all his fullness dwell in him.'

COLOSSIANS 1:15–16, 19

Within a Jewish worldview, such language was far from innocuous. And in due course, the early Christians became clear that, in using this title 'Lord' of Jesus, they were indeed consciously ascribing to him a share in God's identity and activity. Jesus' exaltation to the Father's right hand was a sign that he effectively shared in God's ruling and indeed in his very nature.

This is truly remarkable. After centuries of being schooled in the oneness of Israel's God, these Jewish Christians were confessing Jesus as 'Lord'. They found they were worshipping him. They were also seeing his life and death as the work of God. And they took this radical step because of the resurrection.

The Jewish background

It is often argued, however, that this bold step (of making Jesus to share in God's identity) can only have begun among Gentile Christians – those who did not share these strong Jewish monotheistic convictions. But the evidence is firmly against this.

There is, for example, a phrase preserved from the Aramaic-speaking Jewish Christians which means

Jesus was reunited with the disciples on a 'mountain' in Galilee.

‘O Lord, come’ (*Maranatha*: 1 Corinthians 16:22). Clearly Jewish Christians had been praying to Jesus as ‘Lord’. More striking still is the way Paul in 1 Corinthians reworks the great monotheistic slogan of Judaism (‘Hear, O Israel: The Lord our God, the Lord is one’). Jesus has, as it were, been placed right in the heart of the One God of Israel, sharing his divine identity. Paul and others did not lose their Jewishness when they confessed Jesus as ‘Lord’. They knew what they were doing and the vastness of what it meant.

This radical new understanding of who Jesus was then spreads its way throughout the New Testament. It can be seen in Paul’s first letter (to the Galatians) when he opens with a greeting from ‘God our Father and the Lord Jesus Christ’. This means, as one scholar, Martin Hengel, has put it, that the most important developments in Christology occurred in the first 10 years after the resurrection – before a single word of the New Testament was written. Above all, it comes through in the opening chapters of Colossians, John’s Gospel and Hebrews.

Yet it can be found everywhere; it is taken as a constant working assumption. There is no New Testament writer who does not share this belief that to talk of Jesus is in some profound way also to be speaking about God. Within living memory of the man who had walked on the hills beside Lake Galilee, people are claiming that he was to be identified as the unique son of Israel’s God.

What could possibly make them do it? It was not (as we have seen) because they were wanting to leave their Jewish heritage behind. Nor was it an exercise in ‘one-upmanship’, making out their religious leader to be one better than anyone else’s

‘Yet for us there is but one God, the Father, from whom all things came and for whom we live; and there is but one Lord, Jesus Christ, through whom all things came and through whom we live.’

1 CORINTHIANS 8:6

‘God has spoken to us by his Son, whom he appointed heir of all things, and through whom he made the universe. The Son is the radiance of God’s glory.’

HEBREWS 1:2–3

on the market. It was certainly not in order to feel a bit better about themselves – to have such a belief almost certainly brought more problems and persecutions than comfort. Rather, it was because they were constrained by the evidence.

Once again, the resurrection is central: as Paul writes in his greeting to the church in Rome, Jesus was 'declared with power to be the Son of God, by his resurrection from the dead' (Romans 1:4). Without the resurrection, no one would have dreamed of it; but with the resurrection, a whole new way opened up of understanding who Jesus had been all along – not just the true Messiah, but, yes, even God's true Son. And that title 'Son' then becomes the chief way in which Jesus' followers express this staggering truth. True, the phrase 'Son of God' had already been used within Judaism to refer sometimes to the king, sometimes to righteous people, sometimes to Israel as a nation; but now it was adapted for a new purpose – to speak of the unique relationship that existed between the man Jesus and the God of Israel.

Later explanations of Jesus

Who was this 'God' if Jesus was his 'Son'? How could Jesus be fully human and divine? Later Christians had much work to do, requiring great philosophical expertise. Because Jesus' coming was an unprecedented event, with no ready-made categories available to explain it, they had to use concepts (such as 'incarnation') not yet available in the New Testament period. Yet they were not adding to the New Testament, only trying to explain it. Within their Greek culture they also had to talk much more about Jesus' relationship to the divine being, whereas the New Testament (in its Jewish context) spoke of Jesus sharing in God's activity and identity. Yet it was a different way of making exactly the same point.

Such ideas were provocative at the time, and of course remain so to this day. After all, there's quite a bit of difference between saying that Jesus was a great religious teacher and saying that he was a visitation from the living God to planet Earth.

Claim 4: Jesus the Saviour

Seventh-century mosaic of the loaves and fishes in the church at Tabgha, near the traditional site of Jesus' meeting with the disciples by the lake (described in chapter 21 of John's Gospel).

Finally, Peter clearly emphasized Jesus' role as 'Saviour', the unique bringer of 'salvation', the only one through whom people could experience 'forgiveness of sins'. Jesus had appeared in the life of Israel not to make a display of himself but rather to achieve something for others, to bring about what Israel and the world so vitally needed – forgiveness in the sight of a holy God. According to Peter, Jesus was himself the 'Holy and Righteous One' – a clear hint that he somehow embodied the very holiness of God himself. Yet this same Jesus had endured a painful death. Peter makes quite plain his own belief that Jesus had died according to 'God's set purpose and foreknowledge' and that Christ's sufferings were in keeping with 'all the prophets'. From the outset, the disciples were able to see Jesus' death as something planned by God. And, once again, it is the resurrection alone that can explain this. Without the resurrection Jesus' death was an utter disaster; with it, Jesus' death took on a whole new meaning. Suddenly they had good reason to hope that the tragic recent events in Jerusalem had some purpose.

'God demonstrates his own love for us in this: while we were still sinners, Christ died for us.'

ROMANS 5:8

It may have taken a little while for the full implications to be seen, but Peter's clear preaching of 'forgiveness of sins' in Jesus' name established the framework in which the New Testament authors could soon reach the answer. As Peter would say later in life:

'He himself bore our sins in his body on the tree.'

1 PETER 2:24

'This is love: not that we loved God, but that he loved us and sent his Son as an atoning sacrifice for our sins.'

1 JOHN 4:10

'In him we have redemption through his blood – the forgiveness of sins.'

EPHESIANS 1:7

'Christ died for sins once for all, the righteous for the unrighteous, to bring you to God' (1 Peter 3:18). The New Testament writers saw human wrongdoing as a profound problem, something which made us liable to God's holy judgment. But then they saw that, on the cross, Jesus had dealt with that problem, by bearing that judgment in his own person. The role of Jesus' death in God's plan was to deal with human sin, bringing about the possibility of forgiveness and of 'salvation'. Jesus' death, in other words, was connected not to his own sin (he had none), but rather to ours (the sin of humankind).

The New Testament writers explain this essential link between Jesus' death and our sins in a variety of ways, but the main point is clear enough: Jesus was the one through whom people could receive 'forgiveness of sins' because of his life laid down in death. Sometimes they spoke of his death as a 'sacrifice', sometimes as an act of reconciliation, sometimes as a victory over the powers of death and evil. Yet, whatever the precise wording, there was no doubting that this was the central act of salvation. And so the cross became the centre of their message – not somehow in contrast to the resurrection, but precisely because their belief in Jesus' resurrection threw them back to new and deeper understandings of the cross.

As a result, the followers of Jesus, both past and present, have sometimes been less interested in the earlier parts of Jesus' life. They rush forward to that point where they feel most connected to the story. Paul preached that people are joined to Christ at the point of his death (Romans 6:3) and so is sometimes (wrongly) accused of not being very interested in the earlier parts of Jesus' ministry. But once people become convinced that Jesus truly died for their forgiveness, inevitably they will focus on that death. Jesus' chosen 'memorial' in establishing the Lord's Supper explicitly invites them to do so. This is where people can connect most easily with the story of Jesus.

Conclusion

We asked at the very beginning what could explain Jesus' enduring impact so many years after his cut-short life. We have found our answer in his resurrection. This alone can explain the continuation of the Jesus-phenomenon throughout the last 2,000 years.

For Christians, the resurrection means, above all, that the coming of Jesus was God's ultimate activity in human history. God has written himself into the script of this particular historical narrative in a unique way. There is a living God, they claim, and this is where people can find him. So the story of Jesus can become the story for all people.

The life of Jesus: his ascension

Jesus' final meeting with his disciples was back near Jerusalem, on the Mount of Olives towards Bethany. He told them to wait in the city for the gift of his Holy Spirit, who would then empower them to be Jesus' witnesses 'to the ends of the earth'. 'After he said this, he was taken up before their very eyes and a cloud hid him from their sight' (Acts 1:9). Jesus' ascension is the moment of his return to God, his exaltation to the Father's right hand and the start of his reign over his world. In one sense, it brings his 'life and times' to an end; in another sense, the story is just beginning.

'All authority in heaven and on earth has been given to me. Therefore make disciples of all nations.'

MATTHEW 28:18–19

'Therefore, there is now no condemnation for those who are in Christ Jesus... If God is for us, who can be against us?... Who shall separate us from the love of Christ?'

ROMANS 8:1, 31, 35

Secondly, Christians believe the resurrection means that Jesus is alive. As Paul goes on to say, 'Since Christ was raised from the dead, he cannot die again; death no longer has mastery over him' (Romans 6:9). The resurrection means we are still living in the 'life and times' of Jesus. The real question is no longer 'who was Jesus?' but 'who is this Jesus?' Although Jesus could no longer be seen, all the New Testament writers knew he was a living reality. They could not draw a line in the sands of history and say 'that's where his life ended'.

Many millions ever since have agreed, as they, too, have encountered this risen Jesus. They have then found themselves with a whole new set of priorities: a new allegiance (following Jesus as Lord); a new assurance (of forgiveness and a hope for eternity); a new affirmation (the value they believe God gives to them); a new atmosphere (receiving by faith God's love and joining the community of Jesus' followers); and a new agenda (living out Jesus' kingdom values and spreading the news of Jesus as king).

Finally, because of the resurrection, the New Testament writers became convinced that Jesus was the true Lord of the whole world – indeed that the whole world was, in a profound sense, his. They went so far as to assert that Jesus was also the world's creator in the past and will be its future judge: 'He was in the world, and though the world was made through him, the world did not recognize him' (John 1:10). So at the end of time 'every knee should bow... and every tongue confess that Jesus Christ is Lord' (Philippians 2:10, 11).

'The Word became flesh and lived among us.'

JOHN 1:14

It is a remarkable claim. If true, then 'Jesus and his world' no longer simply refers to the world in which he once lived. It might also mean the world over which he reigns.

Chronology

c. 1003 BC: King David establishes Jerusalem as his capital.

c. 970 BC: Dedication of Solomon's first temple in Jerusalem.

722 BC: Exile of the northern kingdom (Israel) to Assyria.

587 BC: Exile of the southern kingdom (Judah) to Babylon under Nebuchadnezzar.

538 BC: First return from exile under Cyrus.

458 BC: Exiles return under Ezra and then Nehemiah (445 BC).

323 BC: Death of Alexander the Great; Palestine under Ptolemaic rule (Egypt).

198 BC: Palestine under Seleucid rule (Syria).

167 BC: Antiochus IV desecrates the Jerusalem temple.

164 BC: The temple is rededicated after a revolt by Judas Maccabeus; rule of the Hasmonean family.

63 BC: The Roman general Pompey conquers Palestine.

44 BC: Julius Caesar is murdered in Rome.

37 BC: Herod the Great rules Judea.

27 BC: Augustus is proclaimed emperor.

19 BC: Rebuilding of the Jerusalem temple starts.

5 BC: Birth of Jesus (perhaps in the spring), followed by the death of Herod (in March, 4 BC).

AD 6: Archelaus is deposed, leading to Rome's direct rule over Judea and Samaria; revolt of Judas the Galilean.

AD 14: Augustus is succeeded by Tiberius.

AD 26–36: Pontius Pilate, procurator of Judea.

AD 29: Ministry of John the Baptist and Jesus' baptism (Luke 3:23).

AD 30: Jesus' first visit to Jerusalem for Passover (John 2:23).

AD 33: Jesus' crucifixion and resurrection.

AD 34: Saul's conversion on the road to Damascus (Acts 9).

AD 39: Emperor Caligula attempts to have his statue set up in the Jerusalem temple.

AD 41–44: Reign of Herod Agrippa I.

AD 49: Emperor Claudius expels the Jews from Rome.

AD 62: Murder in Jerusalem of Jesus' brother, James.

AD 64: Great fire in Rome and Nero's persecution of Christians; deaths of Peter and Paul.

AD 66: First Jewish revolt against Rome.

AD 70: Fall of Jerusalem to the Romans under Vespasian's son, Titus.

AD 132: Second Jewish revolt against Rome under Simon Bar Khosiba.

Suggestions for Further Reading

R.A. Burridge, *Four Gospels, One Jesus?* SPCK, 1994.

M. Borg and N.T. Wright, *The Meaning of Jesus*, Harper & Row, 1999.

R.T. France, *The Evidence for Jesus*, Hodder & Stoughton, 1986.

S. McKnight, *A New Vision for Israel*, Eerdmans, 1999.

J. Pollock, *The Master: A Life of Jesus*, Hodder & Stoughton, 1984.

M.A. Powell, *Jesus as a Figure in History*, Westminster John Knox, 1998.

P.W.L. Walker, *The Weekend that Changed the World*, Marshall Pickering, 1999.

D. Wenham and S. Walton, *Exploring the New Testament: Gospels and Acts*, SPCK, 2001.

M.J. Wilkins and J.P. Moreland (eds) , *Jesus under Fire*, Paternoster, 1995.

C.J.H. Wright, *Knowing Jesus through the Old Testament*, Marshall Pickering, 1992.

N.T. Wright, *The Original Jesus*, Lion, 1996.

N.T. Wright, *Jesus and the Victory of God*, SPCK, 1996.

N.T. Wright, *The Challenge of Jesus*, SPCK, 2000.

Index

G

H

I

J

K

L

M

N

O

P

Q

R

S

T

V

W

Y

Z

Picture and Text Acknowledgments

Pictures

Picture research by Zooid Pictures Limited and Lion Publishing plc.

AKG – London: pp. 29 (Erich Lessing), 66 (British Library), 101, 110–111 (Peter Connolly), 123 (Erich Lessing), 138 (Pirozzi), 167.

David Alexander: pp. 19, 52, 70–71, 130, 132, 148, 158.

Bridgeman Art Library: pp. 42–43 (Private Collection), 82–83 (National Gallery, London).

Corbis UK Ltd: pp. 6 (Christine Osborne), 47 (Archivo Iconografico, S.A.), 50 (Araldo de Luca), 67 (Bettmann), 78–79 (David Lees), 92 (Archivo Iconografico, S.A.), 176 (Araldo de Luca).

École Biblique et Archéologique Française de Jérusalem, Couvent Saint-Etienne: p. 121.

Hulton/Getty Images: p. 129.

John Rylands University Library of Manchester: p. 38 (reproduced by courtesy of the Director and University Librarian, the John Rylands University Library of Manchester).

Jon Arnold Images: pp. 12–13, 22–23, 58–59, 102–103, 163, 170–71, 178, 181.

Lion Publishing plc: pp. 1 (David Townsend), 14 (David Townsend), 32 (David Townsend), 89 (David Townsend), 102 (David Townsend), 116 (David Townsend), 161 (David Townsend), 183 (John Williams).

Nazareth Village: pp. 4 (D. Michael Hostetler), 24 (Grace Abdo).

Ronald Grant Archive: pp. 142, 150–151 (The Genesis Project).

Sonia Halliday Photographs: pp. 2–3, 7, 17, 26, 41, 53 (Polly Buston), 62, 69 (Sonia Halliday/Laura Lushington), 75 (F.H.C. Birch), 99, 106–107 (DPSimages.com © 2001), 115, 126, 139, 140–141 (Laura Lushington).

Zev Radovan, Jerusalem: pp. 31, 65, 122, 144.

Peter Walker: pp. 25, 86.

Derek West: maps and charts on pp. 9, 20, 61, 149.

Text